BASIC CLERICAL PROCEDURES

RITA MARTIN BA, FFTCom

Senior Lecturer in Office Systems, Leeds Polytechnic

PITMAN

PITMAN PUBLISHING LIMITED
128 Long Acre, London WC2E 9AN

A Longman Group Company

First published in Great Britain 1986

British Library Cataloguing in Publication Data
Martin, Rita
  Basic clerical procedures.
  1. Office practice
  I. Title
  651.3'7   HF5547.5

Text set in Linotron Optima by Oxprint Ltd, Oxford

Printed and bound in Great Britain
at The Bath Press, Avon

ISBN 0 273 02327 6

CONTENTS

Acknowledgements

The author and publishers are grateful to the
following for permission to reproduce
copyright material:

Barclays Bank
Bell and Howell Ltd
Breckon Bland and Associates Ltd
British Rail
British Telecom
Canon (UK) Ltd
IBM UK Ltd
Midland Bank plc
Olivetti UK Ltd
Pitney Bowes plc
Roneo Alcatel
Rotaprint plc
The Controller, Her Majesty's Stationery
   Office
The Post Office

INTRODUCTION

PHILOSOPHY

This book is designed to train students for the types of jobs and duties they would be expected to perform in an office, in a junior clerical capacity. The basic clerical tasks are:

a copying – data, duplicating
b checking – figures, data
c filing and sorting – documents, correspondence
d calculating – manually and by machine
e typing/writing – letters, memos, envelopes, forms and cards
f answering the telephone

Throughout the units there will be an emphasis on numeracy and literacy.

STRUCTURE OF THE BOOK

Tasks and assignments will be set throughout the units and trainees will be encouraged to keep a record of these in a separate folder which may be presented to an employer. A profile sheet will be kept for the teacher/supervisor to sign when the tasks have been completed satisfactorily. This may be shown to an employer.

Memory joggers will be included throughout the units to consolidate and revise learning. There will also be a section '**Decisions! Decisions!**' which is designed to encourage trainees to solve problems and use initiative.

SCENARIO

The trainee is employed as a junior clerk in the head office of a large superstore in Bradford with branches throughout the country. As part of his/her induction course he/she is spending some time in various departments of the organisation.

1 THE MAIL ROOM

This is your first day and you are required to assist in the Mail Room. There are three staff employed on the early shift, 6.00 am to 2.00 pm, and three staff employed on the late shift, 2.00 pm to 10.00 pm. You will be helping with both the incoming and outgoing mail. Your hours of work will be 9.00 am to 5.30 pm. A trainee in this department will work under the guidance of a supervisor or the chief post clerk.

The Mail Room is a central part of most organisations. Mail coming into the company is delivered to the Mail Room, then sorted and distributed to the various departments. This is known as **incoming mail**. Mail to be sent from the company is collected from the various departments, taken to the Mail Room and then sent out. This is known as **outgoing mail**.

In large organisations it is necessary to have rules or procedures for dealing with incoming and outgoing mail so that mail can be dealt with as quickly as possible.

INCOMING MAIL

You may find the following rules helpful:

1 Sort all envelopes and packets. Do not open any marked 'Private' 'Confidential' or 'Personal'.
2 Open each envelope carefully with a paper knife.
3 Take out the contents and attach any enclosures with a stapler.
4 Make sure the envelope is empty.
5 Date stamp each document (but not cheques).
6 Where a cheque or money is enclosed, details should be entered in a special book. This is called a **Remittance Book**.
7 Sort the correspondence into departments or sections and place into trays ready to distribute.
8 Any letters marked 'Private' 'Confidential' or 'Personal' should be placed unopened in the appropriate tray.

★ **Memory joggers**

1 **What is incoming mail?**
2 **What is outgoing mail?**
3 **What would you do with envelopes marked 'Private'?**
4 **What would you do with money received in the post?**

★ **Decisions! Decisions!**

● **What would you do if, when opening the mail, a letter mentioned an enclosure but the sender had forgotten to send it?**
● **What would you do if, when opening the mail, a customer mentioned a cheque for £55 but the cheque was made out for £50?**

Yes, that's right. In both cases you would show the mail to your supervisor pointing out the error or discrepancy.

Remittance book

When money is enclosed in the mail, it is necessary to keep a written record. After the mail has been opened and checked details are entered into a Remittance Book. There is a sample overleaf (Fig 1).

Trainee task 1 (a)

Check the total. Is it correct? Use your calculator.

REMITTANCES BOOK					
Date	Remitter's name	Method of payment	Account No	Amount £	Cashier's signature
21-9	Addis Ltd - Leeds		—	105 50	YTS
''	K Findlay - Hull		5379	70 00	YTS
''	Thompsons Ltd - Ripon		7954	95 00	YTS
''	Kings Hotel - Haworth		—	440 00	YTS
''	K Baird - Bradford		8954	66 50	YTS
	Total			775 50	YTS

Fig 1

Circulating mail

Often in the mail a memo, letter, magazine or leaflet needs to be seen by several departments or people. If there is no urgency you could use a circulation slip (see Fig 2). This is a small printed slip on which names are listed and each person reads the correspondence and then passes it on to the next one and so on.

If the letter needs to be seen quickly by several departments, the most efficient way is to photocopy the entire letter. This is a quick method and it is accurate as it is an exact copy of the letter.

Photocopying mail

Trainee task 2 (a)

If you have access to a photocopier, take a copy of the circulation slip in Fig 2 so you will have a record of who has to see the document.

CIRCULATION SLIP		
Name	Initials	Date
1 J Roberts	JR	7/9/8-
2 B Patel		
3 M Spencer		
4		
5		
6		
Please circulate the attached document quickly		

Fig 2

★ **Memory joggers**

1 **What is a Remittance Book?**
2 **State two methods of dealing with mail which needs to be seen by several people.**

★ **Decisions! Decisions!**

● **What problems might there be when using the circulation slip method?**

- **When an incoming letter needs to be seen by four departments, what can be done to make sure all four departments see the contents of the letter:**

  a **when the matter is urgent?**
  b **when there is no urgency?**

Trainee task 3 (a)

In your own words prepare a list of rules and procedures for dealing with incoming mail.

OUTGOING MAIL

For your sample folder, please collect and read the following leaflets from the Post Office:

- *'Postal Rates – Inland and Overseas'*.
- *'How to send things you value through the post'*.

These leaflets will explain about other common postal services, eg Consequential Loss Insurance and Compensation Fee parcel.

Mail is typed and prepared in the various departments and then taken to the central Mail Room for despatch. You may find the following rules helpful:

1 Collect outgoing mail from departments.
2 Check that the letter has been signed.
3 Check to see that if any enclosures are mentioned they are attached to the letter.
4 Check address on envelope with address on letter if window envelopes are not used.
5 Fold mail carefully and put in envelopes and seal. (If window envelopes are used, check that the address can be seen.)
6 Make up small packets using specially padded envelopes.
7 Make up parcels using strong brown paper, string and sellotape.
8 Where necessary weigh the envelopes and parcels.
9 Place recorded and registered mail to one side. This is dealt with separately.
10 Use franking machine to stamp all other letters, packets and parcels (see page 6).

Fig 3 is a sample of a window envelope:

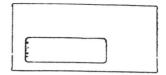

Fig 3

★ **Decisions! Decisions!**

- **What advantage might there be in using window envelopes instead of typing each envelope?**
  Yes, that's right – it is quicker as there is less checking to do.

★ **Memory joggers**

1 **What must you do before mail is put into the envelope?**
2 **If window envelopes are used, what must be checked?**

Trainee task 4 (a)

You have weighed the mail listed below. Using the current postal rates, calculate the correct postage.

Letter Post

Weight not over	1st class	2nd class	Weight not over	1st class	2nd class
60g	17p	12p	450g	78p	59p
100g	24p	18p	500g	87p	66p
150g	31p	22p	750g	£1.28	98p
200g	38p	28p	1000g	£1.70	Not admissible over 750g
250g	45p	34p	Each extra 250g or part thereof	42p	
300g	53p	40p			
350g	61p	46p			
400g	69p	52p			

G Nichols Ltd	2nd class	150 g
P Johnson	2nd class	60 g
Yorkshire Superstores	2nd class	750 g
J Smith – Ripon	1st class	50 g
Inland Revenue	2nd class	1000 g
Leeds Motel	2nd class	250 g
Manchester branch	2nd class	450 g
Garforth branch	2nd class	300 g
Pickerskills Ltd	2nd class	350 g
J Roach – Hull	1st class	100 g

Parcels

There are two rates for parcels:

1 An area rate – this is for local parcels within a group of postal counties.

2   A national rate – this is for parcels outside your group of postal counties.

★ Decisions! Decisions!

- **Your organisation is in Bradford, West Yorkshire. Which other counties are included in the same area rate (see below)?**

★ Memory jogger

1 **What is meant by the area rate for parcels?**
2 **What is meant by the national rate for parcels?**
3 **What categories of outgoing mail are placed on one side and not stamped? (Yes, that is correct. Recorded and registered mail are dealt with separately.)**

Recorded Delivery

Recorded Delivery would be used if you needed proof of posting and a signature upon delivery. It is suitable for sending documents and papers, but not money, jewellery or other valuables, because compensation is limited.

Trainee task 5 (a)

- Find out from the Post Office the current limit of compensation for Recorded Delivery.
- Find out from the Post Office the current fee for Recorded Delivery.

How to use Recorded Delivery

An orange certificate of posting (Fig 4) is filled in and handed over the counter with the letter or packet to the counter clerk, who will date stamp your slip. This is your certificate of posting. The numbered part is gummed on to the letter or packet. You must keep your certificate of posting, in case you have to claim.

When the letter or packet is delivered, it is signed for by the person receiving it and a record is kept by the Post Office.

The Area Rates apply as follows:

County Parcels

For parcels posted and delivered within a group of postal counties as shown below:

1 Avon/Gloucestershire/Somerset/Wiltshire
2 Staffordshire/Warwickshire/West Midlands/Worcestershire
3 Bedfordshire/Leicestershire/Northamptonshire
4 Derbyshire/Nottinghamshire
5 Cambridgeshire/Lincolnshire/Norfolk/South Humberside/Suffolk
6 Dyfed/Gwent/Herefordshire/Mid-Glamorgan/South Glamorgan/West Glamorgan
7 Cheshire/Lancashire
8 Cumbria/Dumfriesshire/Kirkcudbrightshire/Wigtownshire
9 Northern Ireland
10 Berwickshire/East Lothian/Fife/Kinross-shire/Midlothian/Peeblesshire/Roxburghshire/Selkirkshire/West Lothian
11 Aberdeenshire/Banffshire/Kincardineshire
12 Argyll/Arran/Ayrshire/Bute/Clackmannanshire/Coll/Colonsay/Dunbartonshire/Gigha/Iona/Islay/Jura/Lanarkshire/Mull/Renfrewshire/Stirlingshire/Tiree
13 Angus/Caithness/Canna/Eigg/Inverness-shire/Morayshire/Nairnshire/Perthshire/Rhum/Ross-shire/Skye/Sutherland
14 Cleveland/Co Durham/Northumberland/Tyne & Wear
15 North Humberside/North Yorkshire/South Yorkshire/West Yorkshire
16 Berkshire/Buckinghamshire/Oxfordshire
17 Dorset/Hampshire/Isle of Wight
18 East Sussex/Kent/West Sussex
19 Clwyd/Gwynedd
20 Powys/Shropshire
21 Cornwall/Devon
22 Barra/Benbecula/Harris/Lewis/North Uist/South Uist
23 Orkney
24 Shetland

★ Memory joggers

1 For what purposes would you use Recorded Delivery?
2 What must you do at the post office when using Recorded Delivery?
3 What must you keep if you wish to make a claim?
4 What happens when the recorded mail is delivered?

Registered Mail

Registered mail would be used if you wished to send money or other valuable items through the post. All registered mail receives special security throughout its journey.

Money *must* be sent in special envelopes which may be purchased at the Post Office, otherwise compensation will not be paid. Otherwise packets must be strongly packed and fastened with wax or adhesive tape.

The packet must be handed over the counter together with the cost of postage and the registration fee. The counter clerk will give you a certificate of posting which has been stamped. This is your receipt.

When the registered mail is delivered, it is signed for by the person receiving it and a record is kept by the post office.

The current charges are:

Registered Letter Service

The Registered letter service provides for a certificate of posting, delivery against the recipient's signature and special security handling throughout.
First Class Letter Post only

For compensation up to	Fee (in addition to postage)
£ 600	£1.10
£1250	£1.25
£1750	£1.40

Compensation will only be paid for money and certain monetary articles if a registered envelope sold by The Post Office is used. Registration is not a safeguard against damage and compensation for this can only be paid if the contents have been adequately packed. Our leaflets 'How to send things you value through the post' and 'Wrap up well' give further details.

Insurance cover of up to £10,000 against consequential loss is available as an optional extra within the UK only (our leaflet 'Consequential Loss Insurance' gives further details of this facility).

Registered Letter Envelopes

Printed with £1.27 stamp (Registration £1.10, postage 17p)

Stock Letter	Size	Prices including VAT Each	Packet of 10
Small (G)	156mm x 95mm	£1.35	£13.50
Medium (H)	203mm x 120mm	£1.38	£13.80
Large (K)	292mm x 152mm	£1.46	£14.60

A discount of 12p per 100 on the packet rate can be obtained for Registered Letter Envelopes purchased in quantities of 1000 or more. Supplies can be ordered direct from Postal Supply Department, Security Stores Division, Maylands Avenue, HEMEL HEMPSTEAD, Herts HP2 4SF.

This part is affixed to letter or packet

F 544501 Recorded Delivery

Certificate of Posting for Recorded Delivery

How to post

1 Enter below in ink the name and full address as written on the letter or packet.
2 Affix the numbered adhesive label in the top left-hand corner of the letter (or close to the address' on a packet).
3 Affix postage stamps to the letter for the correct postage and Recorded Delivery fee.
4 Hand this certificate, together with the letter, to an officer of The Post Office.
5 This certificate will be date-stamped and initialled as a receipt. Please keep it safely, and produce it in the event of a claim.

Name Mr R A Sharp
Address 17 Kings Road
HARROGATE

◄ Sender completes details

Postcode HG1 4JK
Recorded Delivery should not be used for sending money or valuable items.

For Post Office use Date stamp

Accepting Officer's initials

◄ Counter clerk date stamps here—this is your receipt or Certificate of Posting

Recorded Delivery no.
F 544501

P2297 Apr 84

Fig 4

Trainee task 6 (a)

- The Personnel Department occasionally sends wages to shop-floor workers who are absent from work due to illness. Calculate how much it would cost to send £109 by registered post. The packet weighs 100g and it is to be sent by first class post.
- The Sales Department wishes to send vouchers worth £1500 by registered post. The packet weighs 750g and it is to be sent first class. Calculate the cost.

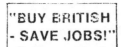

Fig 5

★   Memory joggers

1   For what purpose would you use registered mail?
2   What must you do at the Post Office when using this service?
3   Does this service receive special security throughout its journey?
4   What is the maximum compensation?

Fig 6

★   Decisions! Decisions!

- The Personnel Department wishes to send certificates to successful trainees after the completion of their training. Which service would you recommend and why?
- Trading stamps and vouchers are to be sent to garages. Which service would you use and why?
- A sales representative at a recent sales meeting left his watch in the cloakroom. How will you post it back to him? What service will you use?

A franking machine may be hand or electrically operated. They may be bought or hired and must meet certain conditions laid down by the Post Office.

Postage units are bought in advance from the Post Office. The meter has to be taken to the Post Office where payment is made in advance for an agreed amount of postage. The meter is then pre-set for this amount. As the machine is used it records on a dial the number of units used. At regular intervals the meter is checked and further postage is bought.

It is normally the duty of the trainee to change the date each day on the franking machine, to frank mail, to enter a daily record on the franking machine docket and to keep a watchful eye on when the meter needs resetting. At the end of the week the franking machine docket must be posted to the Post Office from where the units were bought.

Franking machines

As your company is a large organisation a franking machine is used for the outgoing mail.

This is a machine which prints a form of postage stamp and date on envelopes, or on strips of gummed paper for parcels. It may also print the name and address of the firm or an advertising slogan, if desired. (See Figs 5 and 6.)

FRANKING MACHINE CONTROL CARD

User ...*Bradford Superstores Ltd*......................

Machine
(or Meter) No ...*662219*.......... Setting or
Recording Unit ...*1p*.................

Setting Office
(as shown on Record Card) ...*Bradford Main PO*...............

I certify that the following entries for the above machine for the week

ended ...*22 September*...are correct

and that the correct date has been shown on each day's posting.

PLEASE CHECK DATE DAILY

Initial the column below to show date has been changed		ALL MACHINES	LOCKING MACHINES	ALL MACHINES
		Reading of Ascending Register	Reading of Descending Register	Last entry in col. "Total Deposits" or "Total Settings" on Record Card
		(Totalisator)	(Credit Meter)	
AT	Mon.	11000		27000
AT	Tue.	16000		27000
AT	Wed.	26000		27000
AT	Thur.	35000		67000
AT	Fri.	48000		67000
AT	Sat.			

NOTE 1.   This card should be posted on Saturday (or on Friday if no postings are made on Saturday) whether or not the machine has been used in that week.

NOTE 2.   The daily entry must be made on completion of each day's postings.

Signed ...*A Trainee*................

...*22/9/198 -*...

Post Office Examining Officer's initials ....

This is a record of every unit used. Each time mail is franked, the total increases (it is like a mileometer on a car). At the end of the day enter the final reading in this column.

This is the amount of postage which has been bought in advance (pre-paid). This figure is set by the Post Office.

Trainee task 7 (a)

- On the previous Friday the totalisator column read 10 000. You can see from the card that this Friday the reading is 48 000. Calculate how many units have been used this week. If each unit is 1p, what is the cost of postage this week?
- On Thursday extra postage was bought. Calculate how many units were bought. If each unit is 1p, how much did this cost?

★ Memory joggers

1 **List four duties of a trainee when using franking machines.**
2 **What happens to the franking machine docket at the end of the week?**

★ Decisions! Decisions!

- **Why was it decided to buy more units on Thursday? Look at the docket carefully.**
- **Where would you take the franking machine to have the machine pre-set for postage bought in advance?**

Franking machines and new technology

One of the leading manufacturers of franking machines has introduced a franking machine whereby postage may be bought via a computer link to a data centre. This is how it works:

First, the customer must maintain an advance deposit with the manufacturer. This is to cover their purchase of units. When the customer requires more postage, they telephone a special data centre, operated by the manufacturer. Then, using a touch-tone data pad, they enter the account number, meter number and register readings.

A computer controlled voice response system will provide the customer with the resetting number for their meter. This number is then entered into the meter's keyboard. This is known as the **Remote Meter Resetting System**. (See Fig 7.)

Fig 7

CHECK YOUR PROGRESS

1   List the procedures for incoming mail in the correct order:

– take out contents
– distribute to departments
– attach enclosures
– date stamp
– open mail
– deliver 'Private' mail
– take extra copies
– record money received

2   From the procedures above, list the duties of a junior in the Mail Room when dealing with incoming mail.

3   List two methods for dealing with incoming mail when it has to be seen by other departments:

  a   which method is the cheapest?
  b   which method is the quickest?

4   How would you deal with money received in the post?

5   Make a list of rules which would be helpful to a new junior in the Mail Room who is dealing with outgoing mail.

6   What are the duties of a trainee when using franking machines?

7   What is meant by:

  a   an area rate for parcels?
  b   a national rate for parcels?

?   Give instances when you would use Recorded mail. State your reasons.

9   When would you use registered mail, and why?

10 State the equipment which might be used for:

  a   incoming mail, and
  b   outgoing mail

Copy out and *tick* if you are *able* to:

- Outline the procedures for incoming mail
- Deal with mail which needs to be seen by more than one department
- Make a record of money/cheques received in the post
- Outline the procedures for outgoing mail
- Calculate the correct postage for letters and parcels
- Complete a franking machine docket and calculate postage
- State the uses of Recorded and registered mail
- Identify equipment used in the Mail Room
- List the duties of a trainee in the Mail Room

2 FILING

You are now working in the Filing Department. Your duties will be to collect documents, copies, forms, etc ready for filing. You will be required to sort the papers into a definite order, then file them in folders and cabinets ready for use when needed.

CENTRALISED FILING

As Bradford Superstores is a large organisation the majority of the company's papers and documents are kept in one central office and are looked after by filing clerks. This is their sole occupation. They control the lending and borrowing of files and are responsible for the safety and security of files.

Documents and papers are sent to be filed on a daily basis to this central office from the various departments. One of the advantages of centralised filing is that all papers relating to the same subject are filed in the same common file. Another advantage is that everyone has access to the files. This system of filing where there is central control in a central location is known as **centralised filing**.

DEPARTMENTAL FILING

However, certain departments do retain their own filing systems within their departments, eg Personnel, the Director's Office. This is because many of the documents and files are of a confidential nature and should not be available to all staff. This system of filing is known as **departmental filing**. In a smaller organisation or in a small office all files would probably be kept in each office.

★ **Decisions! Decisions!**

● **Why is it necessary to file documents?**

Yes, that's correct – to keep documents safe
– so that you may refer to any document quickly and easily
– so that you may have a written record
– to keep the office clean and tidy

● **Can you identify any disadvantage or problem with centralised filing?**
Yes, your office may be located some distance away from the filing office; also another department may have borrowed the file you need.

★ **Memory joggers**

1 **Differentiate between centralised and departmental filing.**
2 **Identify three advantages to centralised filing.**
3 **Why do certain departments keep their own filing systems?**

CLASSIFICATION OF FILES

There are four main methods of organising or classifying files. These are:

1 Alphabetical
2 Geographical
3 Subject
4 Numerical

9

Chronological filing is the arrangement of documents within a file, in date order. The most recent date goes to the front, and is often combined with other methods of filing.

The most common and simplest form of filing is **alphabetical filing**. This is used for 90% of all filing. A folder is allocated for every individual or firm. There is usually a Guide Card for each letter of the alphabet (Fig 8).

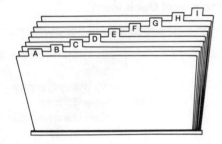

Fig 8

Some letters are broken down even further (Fig 9).

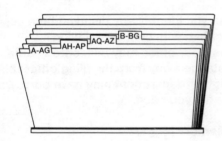

Fig 9

Small amounts of correspondence are kept in a **Miscellaneous** file until there are sufficient documents to justify opening a new file (Fig 10).

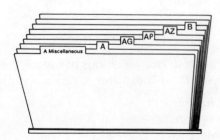

Fig 10

★ **Decisions! Decisions!**
● **What type of documents might be suitable for alphabetical filing?**
● **Why do you think 90% of all filing is filed alphabetically?**
● **What are the advantages of alphabetical filing?**

  Yes, that's right – it is simple and easy to use and understand
  – you can file direct
  – it makes a provision for small amounts of correspondence to be kept in a Miscellaneous file

As 90% of all filing is arranged in alphabetical order it is important to know the main filing rules. These are:

TOP TEN FILING RULES

1   The **surname** rule – file according to the surname, which is considered before the forename or initials, eg:

A Whitham
George Nichols
George Stead
Robert Coster

The correct order should be:

COSTER Robert
NICHOLS George
STEAD George
WHITHAM A

2   The **surname** + **initial** rule – when surnames are the same then file according to initials or names which follow them:

MARTIN A
MARTIN Anne
MARTIN C
MARTIN K M

3   The **nothing before something** rule – when surnames have no initials they are placed before surnames with names and/or initials:

SCHOFIELDS
SCHOFIELDS J
SCHOFIELDS Robert
SCHOFIELDS Ryan

4   The **Mac** rule – names beginning with M (used as a prefix), or Mc or Mac are all treated as names beginning with Mac so that the alphabetical order begins with the letter *after* Mac, eg:

McCALL that is C
MACKENZIE that is K
MACKINSON
M'TAVISTOCK

5   The **Saint** rule – when names contain the word Saint or St they are filed as if the word is spelt out in full, ie Saint:

SAINT E M
ST JAMES' HOSPITAL
ST JOHN–BINNS L
ST MICHAEL'S COLLEGE

6   The **prefix + hyphen** rule – names which have a prefix are filed as if they were a complete word. Names which are hyphenated are treated as if they were a complete word, eg:

DE LA RUE
DE LA TARE
DE VENISE

O'BRIEN
O'CONNELL
O'REILLY

DOLBY–GLOVER
PICTON–TOWERS
SMITH–FORSYTHE

7   The **local authority** rule – file these according to the place or name of the local authority, eg:

BRADFORD Metro
KIRKLEES Works Department
SHEFFIELD City Council

8   The **government department** rule – file according to the name of the department, eg:

EMPLOYMENT, Department of

HEALTH & SOCIAL SECURITY, Department of
WORKS, Department of

9   The **initials** rule – when the name of the company is made up of initials, file according to the alphabetical sequence, eg:

H & C AUTO SPARES
H G V SERVICES
H J T MANAGEMENT SEVICES

except when the initials are being used as an abbreviation for well-known companies or organisations, eg:

AA   – Automobile Association
BR   – British Rail
YTV – Yorkshire Television

10   The **numbers** rule – when the name of a company begins with a number this is spelt out, eg:

7-UP – SEVEN UP
600 Group – SIX HUNDRED GROUP
20th Century Printing –
     TWENTIETH CENTURY PRINTING

Training task 8 (a)

Listed below are items to be filed. Identify the filing rule you will use for each item:

BRADFORD METRO
GERRARD ELECTRICAL LTD
CLIFFORD HAIG LTD
DOLBY-GLOVER & CO LTD
SHABNAM BASHIR
THOS DE LA RUE
DEPARTMENT OF HEALTH & SOCIAL
    SECURITY
F & B REPROGRAPHICS
TARIQUE NASEEM
FAIRWAYS
FAIRWAYS SOFT DRINKS
3-M COMPANY

★   **Memory joggers**

1   **Why is it important to know the main rules governing alphabetical filing?**
2   **How many rules can you remember?**

3   **What is centralised filing?**
4   **What is departmental filing?**

★   **Decisions! Decisions!**

● **Can you think of any disadvantages to alphabetical filing?**
Yes, there might be confusion with common names, eg Brown, Smith and Jones. You would need to pay careful attention to these files. Another disadvantage is that certain files may become bulky, eg there would be more files under the letter B than the letter Z.

RELEASE SYMBOL

When papers or documents are ready to be filed, they are marked with a release symbol. This is usually a tick.

FILING PROBLEMS

Trainee task 9 (a)

One of the problems with alphabetical filing is misfiling files with common surnames. There are several employees named BROWN in your organisation, please rearrange their files in the correct order:

BROWN
BROWN Arthur
J BROWN
Eric BROWN
BROWN Stuart
BROWN Stanley
Janice BROWN
(See also Assignment Book Trainee Task 10 (b) for further practise.)

★   **Decisions! Decisions!**

● **In what order would you file the following:**

DENNIS FISHER, Farrar Lane, Leeds
DENNIS FISHER, Thornhill Place, Bradford
DENNIS FISHER, Clough Street, Halifax
DENNIS FISHER, Windsor Road, Huddersfield

Any ideas? Any suggestions? Did you guess correctly? When identical names have to be filed, deal with the names as usual, then file according to *town*, and if necessary, then *street*.

Trainee task 10 (a)

Rearrange the four names in the correct order.

Filing within the same letter

Another filing problem is misfiling within the same alphabetical letter. Please see Assignment Book Trainee Task 11 (b).

★   **Decisions! Decisions!**

● **Under which letters would you file the following:**

PETER DOMANI WINES
JOHN PETERS FURNISHINGS

Yes, there could be a problem here. If there is any doubt about where to file a document or file, it is placed under the most likely letter of the alphabet and then a notice is placed under the alternative letter. This is known as a *cross-reference*, eg:

PETER DOMANI WINES – if it is decided to file under the letter P, then a note would also be placed in letter D (Fig 11).

```
For DOMANI, PETER WINES
See PETER DOMANI WINES—P file
```

Fig 11

★   **Memory joggers**

1   **What are the four methods of filing?**
2   **Which is the most common method of filing?**
3   **When would you use a cross-reference?**

Trainee task 11 (a)

You are required to make an up-to-date mailing list of store managers. Please rearrange these in alphabetical order:

JIM CONNEL – Belfast
RAY FIRTH – Huddersfield
TOM GRIFFIN – Sheffield
PETER WATSON – Plymouth
GEORGE HUMPHRIES – Wakefield
PETER THORNE – Leeds
MALCOLM WALTERS – Scarborough
JANE LEATHLEY – Bridlington
JOHN LEDGER – Barnsley
JEFF HARE – Ayr
KENNETH HARDY – Bristol
MICK LYONS – Morecambe
ANNE ROBSHAW – Carlisle
JOHN HINCLIFFE – Liverpool
PETER SARGENT – Reading
TOM HARDY – Chesterfield
KEN NAIRN – Cardiff
MARION WALTERS – Newcastle
BRIAN POLLARD – Stockton
RAY STERLING – Halifax

FILING AND COMPUTERS

Many files are now stored on the computer.
The computer can be given a set of
instructions (a program) whereby it will place
the files in the correct alphabetical order. This
is known as a 'sorting' package. The operator
merely keys in the files in any order, then at
the touch of a button, the computer will sort
the files into the correct order.

GEOGRAPHICAL FILING

Geographical filing is a method of arranging
files in alphabetical order according to
location, eg county, town (Fig 12).
Geographical filing is used within Bradford
Superstores for sales territories and location
of stores.

Trainee task 12 (a)

Prepare a list of other types of organisations
who might use geographical filing and state
for what purposes.

SUBJECT FILING

Subject filing is a method of arranging files
in alphabetical order according to subject
(Fig 13).

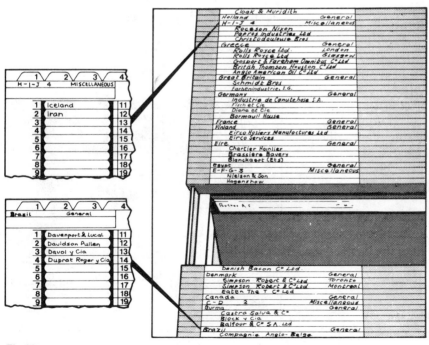

Fig 12

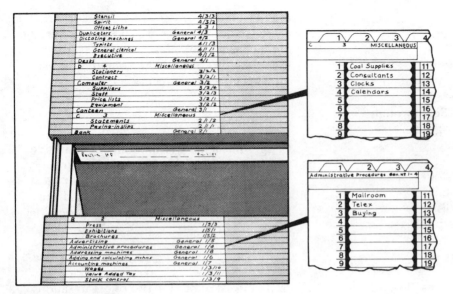

Fig 13

Trainee task 13 (a)

Rearrange the following items in subject order:

Finance
Sales
Purchase
Stores
Credit Control

NUMERICAL FILING

Numerical filing is the method where each item, file or document is given a number. The numbers follow consecutively, ie one after another. This is particularly suitable for filing invoices, orders, requisitions (Fig 14).

Trainee task 14 (a)

Rearrange the following invoice numbers in the correct order, starting with the lowest number first:

493405   696418   634638   628217   689860
650391   463383   451579   792571

If you have a sorting package on the computer, this task can be completed very quickly using the package.

CARD INDEX SYSTEMS

An alphabetical card index system is often used with numerical filing. For example Bradford Superstores issues each employee with a pay number. This is used when clocking in, and subsequently for the calculation and payment of wages. The firm will need to keep a record of pay numbers together with personal details of employees.

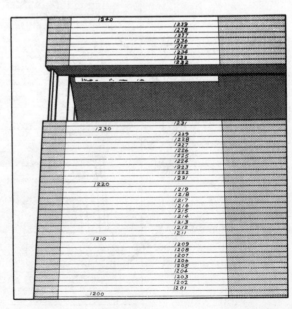

Fig 14

This is usually kept on a separate card and is filed alphabetically. (See Fig 15.)

THOMPSON, PAUL	PAY No. 2945
23 Lulworth Road BRADFORD BD9 8PX	DEPT DIY

Fig 15

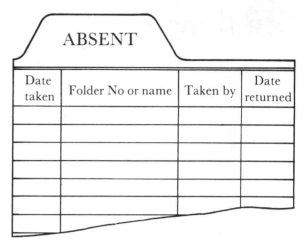

Date taken	Folder No or name	Taken by	Date returned

Fig 16

In your sample folder, complete a card index for J Peterton who works in the warehouse. His pay number is 6033 and his address is 14 Robin Hood Way, Thornton, Bradford BD7 4AB.

★ Decisions! Decisions!

- **If an employee wishes to borrow a file from the central filing office, what records would you recommend be kept?**

    Yes, you would need to know
    – *who* has borrowed the file
    – *what* file has been borrowed
    – *where* it has been taken from (its location)
    – *when* it will be returned

    You would use an *absence card* and place this in the cabinet from where the file had been taken. (See Fig 16.)

In your sample folder, design an absence card to be used when files are borrowed.
Complete this card with the following details:

J Brown of the Order Department wishes to borrow the file marked NMJS Wholesalers Ltd. Use today's date.

FILING EQUIPMENT

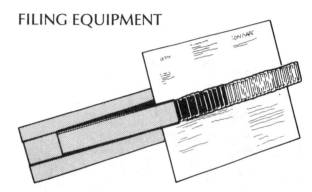

Fig 17

This would be used for pre-sorting files/ documents, before placing them in cabinets.

Fig 18

This would be used for filing cards.

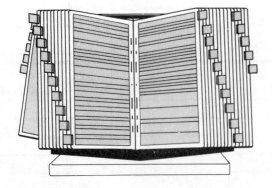

Fig 19

This would be used for filing cards or strips.

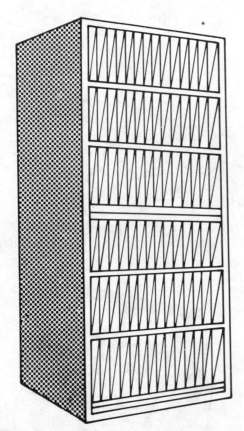

Fig 20

This would be used for documents and folders. Files are placed side by side (saves space). Folders are usually suspended on a rail so that the title strip may be seen. These cabinets may be locked.

Fig 21

Traditionally these cabinets consist of four drawers. Files are placed or hung vertically inside drawers with index cards, titles, etc placed flat on top of files so that they are clearly visible. These cabinets may be locked.

MICROFILMING

Many large organisations avoid having valuable floor space used for storing old files by microfilming their records. The original documents can then be destroyed. When it is necessary to read the document the microfilm is put into a reader. The reader projects and enlarges the film so that it can be easily read. A printout is obtainable on certain readers.

Advantages of microfilming

1   Microfilming can reduce storage space by 98%.
2   Microfilm is more durable than paper.
3   Microfilm is cheaper to send by mail – 60 A4 pages can be contained on a single piece of postcard-size film.
4   Paper copies and duplicates can be made easily.
5   Less risk of misplacing or losing records.
6   Document retrieval is almost instantaneous on a computer assisted system.

Microfilm may be produced in three formats:

• Roll film – two rolls of 16mm microfilm can contain the entire contents of a filing cabinet

- Fiche – normally the size of a postcard and can contain up to 200 documents
- Jacket – this system combines both formats: cut strips of roll film are inserted into a transparent jacket

Microfilm systems

1 **Reader system** – this is a basic reader used for reading microfilm only.
2 **Camera/Reader system** – this gives the capability of generating your own film.
3 **Camera/Reader/Processor system** – this system is designed for companies who wish to process their own film. Microfilm would be kept on the premises at all times.
4 **Camera/Mini-computer/Reader/Processor system** (See Fig 22).

For high-speed indexing of documentation, mini-computer-based systems are available. They allow documents to be indexed as they are filmed, and mean that any document can be retrieved virtually instantly.

★ **Memory joggers**

1 What are the advantages of using microfilm?
2 What are the three formats of producing microfilm?
3 Explain the four microfilm systems and the equipment which would be used.

★ **Decisions! Decisions!**

- Can you suggest any disadvantages to using microfilm?

★ **Memory joggers**

1 What do you understand by geographical filing?
2 For what purposes would you use subject filing?
3 What is the main advantage of numerical filing? Are there any disadvantages?

★ **Decisions Decisions!**

- Which method of filing would you recommend for the following:

  a correspondence received from customers
  b invoices from suppliers
  c personnel records
  d price lists and catalogues
  e orders sent to suppliers
  f sales figures from various territories

  Give your reasons.

- Which filing equipment would be most suitable for:

  a lists of telephone numbers
  b catalogues, price lists
  c sorting out a back-log of invoices
  d correspondence from regular customers?
  e card index system giving details of employees
  f confidential files on employees

Give your reasons

Fig 22

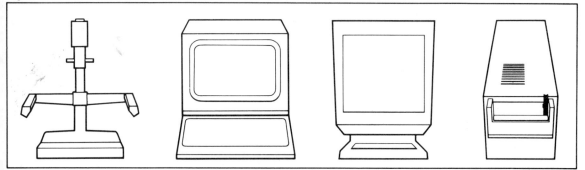

CONFIDENTIAL FILES

Many files are now stored on the computer on a **database**. This is a store of information structured in such a way that the operator can quickly locate data. Many confidential records are now stored on computers for security reasons. To access the record or file a password has to be used. As more and more information is transferred from traditional files on to the computer, security and confidentiality is becoming increasingly important. The password system is only effective as long as the password does not fall into the wrong hands.

CHECK YOUR PROGRESS

1   State four reasons why it is necessary to file documents/papers.
2   When should you do the filing (tick the correct answer):

once a week
every month
daily – first thing each morning
save it up until you have a lot

3   Files can be kept in a central filing room, or they can be filed .... ?
4   Explain the four main methods of filing.

5   Nearly 90% of all filing is arranged .... ?
6   Which method of filing requires a card index and why?
7   When papers are ready to be filed the employer puts on the paper a sign. It is called a (tick the correct answer):

cross reference
absence card
release symbol

8   Explain by giving two examples how you would file documents with the same name.
9   How many of the Top Ten filing rules can you remember? Give examples for each one.
10   List the duties of a junior filing clerk.

Copy out and *tick* if you are able to:

- File alphabetically
- File geographically
- File in subject order
- File numerically
- Use absence cards
- Use cross-reference cards
- Understand and apply the main filing rules
- Identify equipment used in the filing department
- List the duties of a trainee in the filing department

3 THE GENERAL OFFICE

You are now working in the General Office. Your duties will be to type routine correspondence and forms, to take messages, to help with the issue of stationery and general office duties as required by senior secretaries and typists.

In your sample folder, please collect samples of:

A4 stationery
A5 stationery
Letterheads from various business
   organisations
Forms
Standard letters

CORRESPONDENCE

Memoranda

A memorandum is used for internal communication within the company. This is for correspondence between departments, sales representatives, staff. A memorandum is a printed form wherein the typist completes the information. (See Fig 23.)

Illustrated overleaf (Fig 24) is a standard memorandum issued to staff giving details of Bank holiday dates.

Trainee task 15 (a)

You are required to complete a memorandum form informing staff about the Christmas holidays. The offices will close at 12 noon on Christmas Eve (state the day) and will re-open at 9.00 am on 27 December (state the day).

Trainee task 16 (a)

Draft memorandum from the Office Manager to all staff in the General Office informing them of a new Savings Scheme which is to

---

Memorandum

From: Office Manager   **Ref.** DF/REM

To: All Staff — Stores   **Date** 1 March 19--

FIRE DRILL

A fire drill practice is to be held on Monday next at approximately 11.00 am. Staff are requested to follow recommended procedures and keep to recognised exits when leaving the building.

D.F

← No salutation is required

← No complimentary close is used. Sender may initial if he wishes

Fig 23

MEMORANDUM

From	Office Manager	Ref.	DF/REM
To:	All Staff — General Office	Date	19 August 19..

Subject   AUGUST BANK HOLIDAY

Will staff please note that all offices will close at 5.30 pm on Friday 23 August and re-open after the Bank Holiday on Tuesday 27 August at 9.00 am.

D·F

Fig 24

start next month. If staff wish to join the scheme they should contact the Office Manager as soon as possible. Enclose details of the scheme. (See Assignment Book Task 16 (b) for further details.)

★ **Memory joggers**

1   What is a memorandum?
2   How does it differ from a letter?

Letters

Letters may be sent to customers, clients, wholesalers, agents, government departments and so on – in other words, they are sent to persons or organisations outside the firm.

They are often the first impression that an outsider receives of the firm. Therefore a letter should be clearly and politely worded and well-typed and displayed. (See Fig 25.)

Trainee Task 17 (a)

Cover over the arrows and information shown on Fig 25 and identify the following parts of a letter:

– designation
– salutation
– subject heading
– body
– reference
– from whom is the letter?
– to whom is the letter?

★ **Decisions! Decisions!**

● **Differentiate between a letter and a memorandum.**
● **Explain in your own words when you would send a letter and when you would send a memorandum.**

Leeds Polysec Centre

Park Place   Leeds LS1 2SY

Reference → Our ref DS/REM

Date → 25 February 19..

Addressee
(who the
letter is
sent to) →
Mr D Flint
Office Manager
Bradford Superstores
Kings Road
BRADFORD
BD9 8PL

Salutation → Dear Sir

Subject
heading → WORD PROCESSING

We have pleasure in enclosing details of
our new range of word processors.

Body or
main text
of the
letter →
As you will appreciate word processing
has a tremendous potential to streamline
and improve the overall secretarial and
administrative procedures at all levels
in your company.

We should be pleased to arrange a
demonstration of our new models at any
time convenient to you. If you are
interested, please telephone to arrange
an appointment.

Complimentary
close → Yours faithfully

D Shepherd
Designation → Sales Manager

Enclosures → Enc

Fig 25

Envelopes

These are usually typed in the following way:

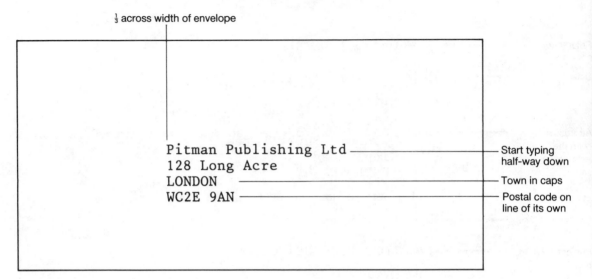

⅓ across width of envelope

Pitman Publishing Ltd —————————— Start typing half-way down
128 Long Acre
LONDON ———————————————— Town in caps
WC2E 9AN ——————————————— Postal code on line of its own

★ **Decisions! Decisions!**

• **Why is it recommended to start typing the address half-way down the envelope?**
• **Many firms use window envelopes for their mail. What advantages might there be in using these envelopes? Are there any disadvantages?**

Standard letters

When correspondence refers to standard situations, eg non-payment of account, non-delivery of orders, it is useful to have a standard letter which can be duplicated or stored on the word processor. The typist then completes the letter with individual details.

The Accounts Department is short staffed and busy so they have sent some of their routine work to the General Office. Fig 26 illustrates a standard letter which is sent to customers who are late settling their account. If you have access to a word processor, this standard letter can be keyed-in and stored for future use.

Trainee task 18 (a)

Please send the standard letter to the following customers who are overdue in settling their accounts.

1 Mr J Watson
   Watson & Baker Ltd
   Call Lane
   LEEDS 1   Invoice No 454581 for £898.36

2 Cusack & Bednall
   230 Long Lane
   TODMORDEN   Invoice No 456969 for £234.69

★ **Memory joggers**

What is a standard letter?

★ **Decisions! Decisions!**

• **Explain in your own words the advantages of using standard letters.**

Trainee task 19 (a)

Type a memo from the Canteen Manager to all staff informing them that the prices in the canteen will be increased by 10% as from Monday next.

TELEX

Bradford Superstores uses the telex service very frequently to contact its branches.
   The telex service provided by British

Dear

According to our records, your Invoice No.   is 2 months
overdue.

Most of our customers appreciate a friendly reminder of an
overdue account because they understand the importance of
maintaining a good credit rating.

No doubt this is an oversight on your part and we would ask you
to give this matter your prompt attention. We look forward to
receiving your cheque for   in the near future.

If you have recently settled your account, please disregard
this notice.

Yours sincerely

R MARTIN
CREDIT MANAGER

Fig 26

Telecom uses teleprinters. This service enables subscribers to rent a teleprinter so that they can contact other telex subscribers anywhere in the world.

A teleprinter is a machine which resembles a typewriter keyboard with a telephone dial. Some teleprinters now use microprocessors to transmit, receive and store messages. The telex service provides a written communication at the speed of a telephone call. (See Fig 27 overleaf.)

How it works

- the operator dials the telex number of firm to be contacted
- a signal is received when the connection is made (there is no talking)
- the operator then types the message on his/her teleprinter which is reproduced at the same time on the teleprinter receiving the message

★ **Decisions! Decisions!**

- **Explain the two main advantages of the telex service.**

Yes, that's right, there is a written record and telex is a speedy means of communication.

Other advantages of Telex

1 It is generally cheaper to use telex than to make a telephone call.
2 Many messages can be prepared in advance. Using the latest technology, which has a word processing facility, messages can be prepared and stored, then recalled when the operator is ready to transmit them.
3 Provided a machine is switched on it can receive messages at any time without the operator being there.

★ **Decisions! Decisions!**

- **Why is it an advantage to be able to receive messages without the operator being there?**
  Yes, that's right, it frees the operator for other work, eg answering the telephone. Also messages can be received when the

Fig 27

firm is closed. Messages can be received overnight ready to be dealt with when the office opens in the morning. This is very useful in communicating with overseas countries where there is a time difference.

Trainee task 20 (a)

Prepare a reply to the telex message from the Newcastle branch (Fig 28) stating that coffee and bin liners will be despatched today by road. You are unable to deliver turkeys – they are out of stock due to the Christmas rush. These will be delivered direct from the supplier on Friday.

Keep your message brief.

★ **Memory joggers**

1 What is a teleprinter?
2 What is the telex service offered by British Telecom?
3 How can messages be prepared in advance?
4 What is the advantage of this?

TELEPHONE CALLS

Although it is often cheaper to use telex the telephone is still frequently used in business. The charge for a call is made up of units. The number of units for each call depends on *when* you make the call and to *where* you make the call.

```
85-07-17   12:01
Msg 122 Title: DH1

55261 BRADSTORES
64429 BRADNC
0945      5/12/84

ATTN FOOD BUYING OFFICE

PLEASE DELIVER

60 X 12 COFFEE JARS - 200G
40 X 12 BIN LINERS - BLACK
100 9 LB FROZEN TURKEYS

REQUIRED ASAP

REGARDS

MARION WALTERS,
STORE MANAGER
NEWCASTLE

64429 BRADNC
25151 BRADSTORES
```

Fig 28

There are three call rates which relate to different times of the day and week – Peak, Standard and Cheap.

Peak rate	9.00 am – 1.00 pm Monday to Friday
Standard rate	8.00 am – 9.00 am and 1.00 pm – 6.00 pm Monday to Friday
Cheap rate	6.00 pm – 8.00 am Monday to Friday and all day/all night at weekends.

Trainee task 21 (a)

Prepare a memo from the Office Manager to all staff asking for their cooperation in saving costs. Indicate the three rates available and ask staff to avoid making calls at the peak time, except in an emergency.

★ **Memory joggers**

1 When is the most expensive time to make a telephone call?
2 When is the least expensive time?
3 What other factor decides the cost of a call? Find out from your telephone directory the three basic categories based on distance.

New technology and telephones

Illustrated below (Fig 29) is the Facilityphone 200 the latest development offered by British Telecom.

Fig 29

This telephone has six important functions:

1 Quick one-button dialling – can store up to 16 numbers in its memory.
2 Has an integral calculator which you can use while talking on the telephone.
3 Has a digital clock.
4 Has a built-in alarm call.
5 Has a call-timer so that you can check on the duration of calls.
6 Has a loudspeaking facility – other parties in the room can be included in the conversation.

CONTROL OF STATIONERY

You are helping one of the senior typists to issue stationery to staff. Each item of stock has a separate stock card. Each time stationery is issued or received from the supplier a record must be made on each card.

Illustrated below (Fig 30) is the stock card for shorthand notebooks.

Trainee task 22 (a)

From the stock card illustrated below (Fig 30):

- Name the supplier of the notebooks.
- What is the present stock?
- What is the minimum stock?
- What is the maximum stock?
- How many should you re-order?
- How many books have been issued throughout the period to the General Office?

- How many books have been issued to the Typing Pool?

★ **Decisions! Decisions!**

- **Why is it necessary to control stock and to keep records?**
- **What is the purpose of *Maximum* and *Minimum* on stock record cards?**

REFERENCE BOOKS

A good clerk is not expected to know everything but should know where and how to obtain information.

Listed below is a list of general reference books to be found in most offices:

Post Office Guide
Telephone directories/The Phone Book
Yellow Pages
AA/RAC books
Dictionary

Fig 30

STATIONERY STOCK CARD

Item: Shorthand Notebooks   Max: 50

Supplier: Office Supplies Ltd   Min: 10

Park Square, Bradford

RECEIPTS			ISSUES			BALANCE
Date	Invoice No	Quantity Received	Date	Quantity Issued	Department 4	Quantity
10.9	4301	50				50
			12.9	6	Gen. office	44
			1.10	5	Secretaries	39
			6.10	8	Typing pool	31
			13.10	7	Secretaries	24
			30.10	4	Gen. office	20
			15.11	2	Mr Wright	18
			19.11	4	Typing pool	14
			24.11	6	Gen. office	8
			25.11	1	Mr Wright	7

Encyclopaedia/*Whitaker's Almanack*
BR timetables
Street directories
Who's Who
Telex directories
Post codes

★ **Decisions! Decisions!**

● **In which reference book(s) would you find the following information:**

   a **street maps listing names of residents**
   b **personal details about a famous person(s)**
   c **how to send a parcel to Kenya**
   d **road map listing motorways and towns**
   e **a list of office equipment suppliers in your area**
   f **the meaning of ARIBA**
   g **weather and road reports**
   h **statistical information obtained from government departments**
   i **times of trains**
   j **hotels and garages in a particular town**

Trainee Task 23 (a)

The General Manager is going away on business and has been recommended to stay at the following hotels:

a The Westmoreland Hotel, London, NW8
b The Beaufort Hotel, Bath
c The Savoy Hotel, Bournemouth

Find out what facilities each of these hotels has to offer. Do not worry about the charges, they will probably have changed anyway!

CHECK YOUR PROGRESS

1 Write out the following sentence, inserting the correct words:
   A memorandum is used for internal/external communication within/outside the company.
2 What is a standard letter?
3 What is the correct method of typing an envelope and why?
4 What are window envelopes and why are they used?
5 What is a teleprinter?
6 List the advantages of the telex system.
7 What records would you recommend be kept when receiving and issuing stock.
8 What times of day do the following telephone charges apply:

   Cheap rate
   Standard rate
   Peak rate

9 List the more common reference books to be found in the General Office. Indicate their contents.

Copy out and *tick* if you are able to:

● Compose and type a memo
● Compose and type a letter
● Complete a standard letter with variable information
● Address an envelope correctly
● Perform routine typing tasks
● Perform routine clerical tasks
● Enter details on stock control records
● Prepare a telex message
● Use basic reference books
● List the duties of a trainee in the General Office

4 ACCOUNTS

You are now working as a trainee in the Accounts Department. Your duties will be checking figures, calculating, listing and pricing items.

CHEQUES

You need to understand the information given on a cheque in order to identify any errors on cheques received in the post. (See Fig 31.)

Refer to drawer

This is when a cheque is referred back to the person who issued the cheque, ie the drawer. There may be several reasons for this:

- there may be insufficient funds in the drawer's account
- the cheque may be post-dated (dated for a future date) – the bank will not pay until then

- the words and figures do not agree
- the cheque is left unsigned
- alteration has not been initialled by the drawer
- incorrect date
- out of date, ie more than six months old

★ Memory joggers

1 **Who is the payee on a cheque?**
2 **Who is the drawer?**
3 **Who is the drawee?**

In order to accept a cheque for payment a cheque must be:

- correctly dated
- made payable to payee
- words and figures should agree
- should be signed
- any alteration should be initialled

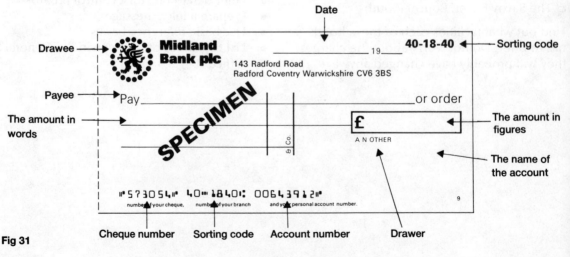

Fig 31

Trainee task 24 (a)

Four cheques have been witheld in the morning's post (see below and page 30). Identify the errors on each cheque.

PAYING IN

In order to pay in sums of money and cheques into a current bank account a paying-in slip must be completed. (See Fig 32, page 31.)

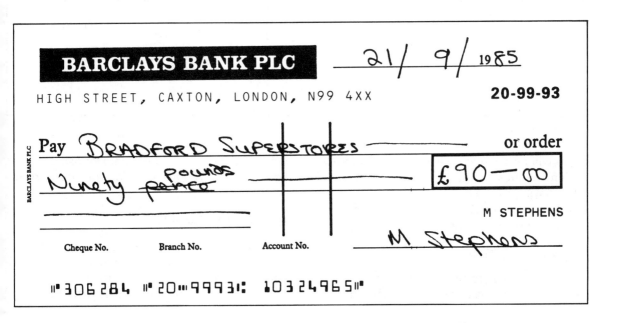

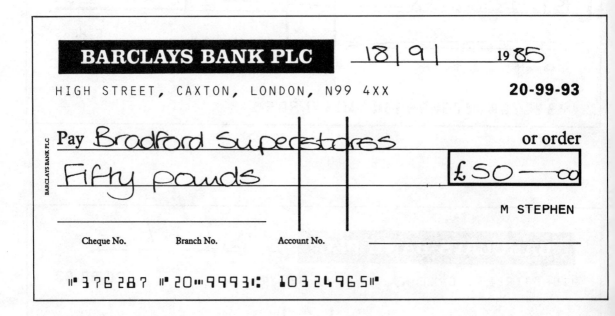

You will notice that cash is listed separately from cheques. Cheques are listed individually. The paying-in slip must be *dated* and *signed* and the counterfoil must be completed so that there is a written record of the amount paid in.

Trainee task 25 (a)

Use your calculator to total the amount of cash and cheques to be paid in. This figure would be entered in the Total Deposit £ column and a record made on the counterfoil.

BANK STATEMENT

The bank periodically issues a statement to each of its customers. This statement indicates each time money is paid into the account (credit) and each time money is withdrawn

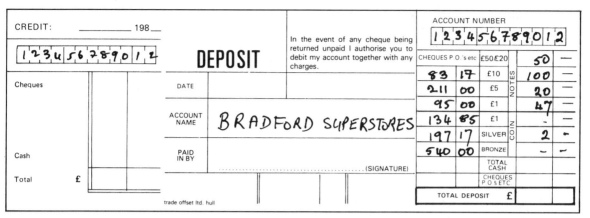

Fig 32

from the account (debit). A balance is shown at the completion of each transaction. (See Fig 33.)

Trainee task 26 (a)

From the bank statement shown in Fig 33 calculate the following:

- How much has been paid in during this period?
- How much has been paid out during this period?
- What was the balance at the beginning of the period?
- What is the final balance?

★ **Memory joggers**

1 **What form is used to pay in money or cheques into a current account?**
2 **What must you check when checking a cheque?**
3 **What is the purpose of a bank statement?**

★ **Decisions! Decisions!**

- **Although the final balance is shown on the statement, this may not be the correct amount. Why is this?**
 Yes, one of the reasons is that cheques may not have been cleared, ie passed for payment, and are therefore not shown on the statement.
- **How may the correct balance be obtained?**
 Yes, that's right, you would have to check your paying-in book and cheque counterfoils. This is known as reconciling the statement.

PETTY CASH

In the office it is convenient to pay small amounts in cash from money that is available for this purpose, ie the petty cash. Fares, gratuities, office cleaning materials and other miscellaneous small items are usually paid for out of petty cash.

Date	Code	Reference	Debit	Credit	Balance
12.8					162.72
15.8	CHQ	001597	29.68		133.04
17.8	CHQ	001601	23.00		110.04
18.8	CHQ	001602	14.50		95.54
19.8	CC	J Robinson		715.68	811.22
20.8	CHQ	001604	405.00		406.22

Fig 33

If there are many small payments they will be dealt with by the cashier, otherwise a secretary or other member of staff may be responsible.

A strict record of all petty cash payments should be kept. Every person to whom petty cash is paid should sign a dated receipt or a petty cash voucher.

Details of the expenditure should be written or typed on the voucher. If there is additional evidence of the amount spent, such as a stationer's receipt, it should be attached.

Staff requiring repayment of personal money spent on behalf of the firm are usually required to write out and sign a petty cash voucher. This is a receipt for the money received from the petty cashier. All signed petty cash vouchers should be kept in the petty cash box.

★ Memory joggers

1   **What sort of items are usually paid out of petty cash?**
2   **What information is contained on a petty cash voucher?**
3   **Where are petty cash vouchers usually kept?**

Trainee task 27 (a)

Using the voucher below, state:

- What is the purpose of a petty cash voucher?
- What was the item of expenditure?
- Who authorised payment?
- How much was the petty cash voucher for?
- Who received the payment?

Imprest system

Most petty cash is kept on an imprest system. A convenient round sum, such as £10, £20 or £50 is available for cash payments. This is the imprest and is sometimes referred to as 'float' money.

As items are bought a petty cash voucher is completed in order to reclaim money. Details are then entered into the petty cash book.

Petty cash vouchers are usually numbered consecutively in the order they are received. The details and number on each voucher are then entered in the petty cash book. The petty cash book is ruled with a total column, followed by a number of analysis columns. (See Fig 34.)

Petty Cash Voucher	Folio		*No 23*	
	Date		18/1/85	
Required for	VAT amount		Amount including VAT	
	£	p	£	p
Tin of coffee – Accounts Department	–	–	£6	50
Total	–	–	£6	50
Signature *B. Thompson*				
Authorised by *J. Smith*				

Restoring the balance

Before all this sum has been spent, a cheque is drawn for the expenditure to date. This cheque is cashed at the bank and the money added to the balance in hand, thus restoring the original amount of cash held. To prevent unauthorised persons tampering with the petty cash, it is usually kept locked in a cash box.

Dr						PETTY CASH BOOK											Cr	
Received		Date	Fo	Details	V No	Total paid out		Stationery		Office expenses		Travel		Postage		VAT		
£						£		£		£		£		£		£		
5	00	7.1		Balance														
15	00	7.1		Cash														
		7.1		String	20		50		50									
		7.1		Tea	21	1	60			1	60							
		9.1		Oxfam donation	22	5	00									5	00	
		10.1		Reg'd letter	23	1	26							1	26			
		11.1		Train fare	24	7	50					7	50					
						15	86		50	1	60	7	50	1	26	5	00	
		11.1		Balance		4	14											
						20	20											
4	14	14.1		Balance														
15	86	14.1		Cash														

Fig 34

Trainee task 28 (a)

Dr						PETTY CASH BOOK											Cr	
Received		Date	Fo	Details	V No	Total paid out		Stationery		Office expenses		Travel		Postage		VAT		
£						£		£		£		£		£		£		
14	00	31.12		Balance														
36	00	31.12		Cash														
		2.1		Plant	1	7	50							7	50			
		10.1		Fares	2		50						50					
		17.1		Paper clips	3	1	20	1	20									
		18.1		Window cleaning	4	5	00			5	00							
		23.1		Taxi	5	2	80					2	80					
		29.1		Tin of coffee	6	6	50							6	50			
		30.1		Telephone cleaning	7	11	50			10	00					1	50	

- The example above is kept on the imprest system. Explain this.

- How will petty cash vouchers be filed?

- What is the amount of petty cash float?
- What was the total amount spent during the period? Use your calculator.
- How much is required at the end of the period to make up the float. Use your calculator.

★   **Memory joggers**

1   **What is the main purpose of the petty cash book?**
2   **What should the cash remaining, plus the current vouchers always total?**
3   **Where is the petty cash money kept?**

Petty Cash Voucher

Folio: 1

Date 1 — 2

Required for	VAT amount		Amount including VAT	
	£	p	£	p
MILK	—	—	£1	50
Total			£1	50

Signature   T. Ainsworth
Authorised by   J. Smith

Petty Cash Voucher

Folio: 4

Date 3 — 2

Required for	VAT amount		Amount including VAT	
	£	p	£	p
Magazines for reception			2	50
Total			2	50

Signature   T. Bedford
Authorised by   J. Smith

Petty Cash Voucher

Folio: 2

Date 2 — 2

Required for	VAT amount		Amount including VAT	
	£	p	£	p
Train fare to Sheffield			7	80
Total			7	80

Signature   L Kenworthy
Authorised by   J. Smith

Petty Cash Voucher

Folio: 5

Date 4 — 2

Required for	VAT amount		Amount including VAT	
	£	p	£	p
Airmail letters	—	—	1	65
Total			1	65

Signature   D. Child
Authorised by   J. Smith

Petty Cash Voucher

Folio: 3

Date 2 — 2

Required for	VAT amount		Amount including VAT	
	£	p	£	p
Plants for reception			5	55
Total			5	55

Signature   T. Clough
Authorised by   J. Smith

Petty Cash Voucher

Folio: 6

Date 8 — 2

Required for	VAT amount		Amount including VAT	
	£	p	£	p
Floor Polish 2 tins @ 90p each	—	—	1	80
Total			1	80

Signature   C Jinks
Authorised by   J. Smith

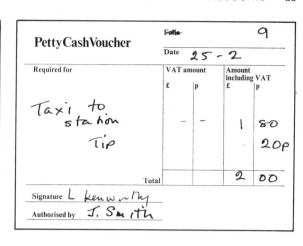

Petty Cash Voucher		Folio		7
		Date	10 – 2	
Required for		VAT amount £	p	Amount including VAT £	p
Office Cleaning		–	–		
				10	00
	Total			10	00
Signature J. Hobson					
Authorised by J. Smith					

Petty Cash Voucher		Folio		9
		Date	25 – 2	
Required for		VAT amount £	p	Amount including VAT £	p
Taxi to station		–	–	1	80
Tip				.	20p
	Total			2	00
Signature L Kenworthy					
Authorised by J. Smith					

Petty Cash Voucher		Folio		8
		Date	11 – 2	
Required for		VAT amount £	p	Amount including VAT £	p
Registered letter		–	–	2	34
	Total			2	34
Signature T. Bedford					
Authorised by J. Smith					

★ **Decisions! Decisions!**

● A junior colleague asks for your help as he/she is unable to balance the petty cash book. The total amount paid out is not the same as the total amount of the analysis columns.

The petty cash vouchers are shown on pages 34–5. Illustrated below is the petty cash book. Check through the vouchers and the petty cash book to decide where the errors have been made. Explain these to your colleague.

Dr				PETTY CASH BOOK							Cr
Received	Date	Fo	Details	V No	Total paid out	Stationery	Office expenses	Travel	Postage	VAT	
£					£	£	£	£	£	£	
12. 00			Balance								
28. 00			Cash								
	1.2		Milk	1	1. 50		1. 50				
	2.2		Fares	2	7. 80			7. 00			
	2.2		Plants	3	5. 55						
	3.2		Magazines	4	2. 50					2. 50	
	4.2		Stationery	5	1. 65	1. 65					
	8.2		Floor polish	6	1. 80					. 90	
	10.2		Office cleaning	7	10. 00		10. 00			10. 00	
	11.2		Registered letter	8	2. 34				2. 43		
	25.2		Taxi	9	1. 80			1. 80		. 20	
					34. 94	1. 65	11. 50	8. 80	2. 43	13. 60	

Did you spot the following errors?

> Voucher No 2 – incorrect total in 'Travel'. It
> should be £7.80 and not
> £7.00.
>
> Voucher No 3 – entered in total column but
> not entered in 'Sundries'
>
> Voucher No 6 – incorrect figure entered in
> 'Sundries'
>
> Voucher No 7 – entered twice, once in
> 'Office Expenses' and
> again in 'Sundries'
>
> Voucher No 8 – amount for £2.34 but
> transposed in 'Postage'
> to £2.43
>
> Voucher No 9 – incorrect amount in the
> 'Total' column

EXPENSES

Employees who have to travel on behalf of the
company are entitled to claim for all expenses.
There is a set scale for these expenses:

Hotel	£20–£30 per night inc VAT
Breakfast	£2.50
Lunch	£4.00
Dinner	£7.00
Train fare	2nd class
Petrol allowance	27p per mile
Subsistence	£4 per day, if absent for more than 24 hours

**ALL CLAIMS TO BE SUBSTANTIATED
BY RECEIPTS**

Trainee task 29 (a)

Mr Howard has to visit the branch at
Newcastle. He has made rough notes for his
visit (see below) and would like you to
prepare an estimated costing for his visit.
What is the total estimated cost for this visit?

Notes for Bradford/Newcastle Visit – 16/17 January

January 16   Bradford/Newcastle by car – 100 miles.
Lunch – Kings Hotel, Newcastle.
Visit store to 7.00 pm.
Dinner at hotel.
Staying at Kings Hotel (£25 per night)

January 17   Breakfast at hotel.
Visit store.
Lunch.
Newcastle/Bradford by car – 100 miles
Dinner at Wetherby Motel.
+ 1 day's subsistence.

INVOICES

An invoice is a bill requesting payment for goods ordered. Most of the company's invoices are prepared on the computer.

However, there have been some special sales promotions in the store. Bradford Superstores rent out space to suppliers who wish to promote their own products. One of the suppliers has purchased goods from the store on credit, therefore an invoice must be issued. (See Fig 35.)

Trainee task 30 (a)

- Calculate the total.
- Who is the buyer?
- Who is the seller?

INVOICE

No 4598

From: Bradford Superstores
Kings Road
BRADFORD
BD9 8PL

Tel: 234567 BRADSTORES

Telex: 55261 BRADSTORES

VAT Registration No 1234 5678

Date: 2 March 1985

To: Yorkshire Cheeses Ltd
High Street
Halton
LEEDS
LS15 8PL

Terms:

Completion of Order No 5734 dated 25 February

Quantity	Description	Cat No	Price each £	Cost £	VAT rate %	VAT amount £
1 case	French red wine	2245	28	28.00		
4 cases	French white wine	2243	25	100.00		
2 cases	Rose wine	2244	26	52.00		
				180.00		
	Plus VAT @ 15%			27.00	15	27.00
E & EO						

Delivered on:
by:

Fig 35

BASIC BUSINESS TRANSACTION

Listed below (Fig 36) are the basic stages in a simple business transaction.

Trainee task 31 (a)

From the chart below:

- Which documents are sent by the buyer?
- Which documents are sent by the seller?
- Which document does the buyer receive when he has bought the goods?
- How does the buyer find out details of the price of goods?
- When the buyer decides to buy, what does he send to the supplier or seller?
- What is the final document in a basic business transaction?

USE OF COMPUTERS IN PREPARING INVOICES

1   A database, which is a store of information, can be created on the computer. This database will contain all details regarding each individual customer, eg name, address, account number, credit rating and discounts allowed.

2   A further file containing details of all stock would be contained within this database, eg prices, description and reference numbers.

3   The operator keys in the information for a particular invoice, eg quantity ordered, name of customer. This is known as the input.

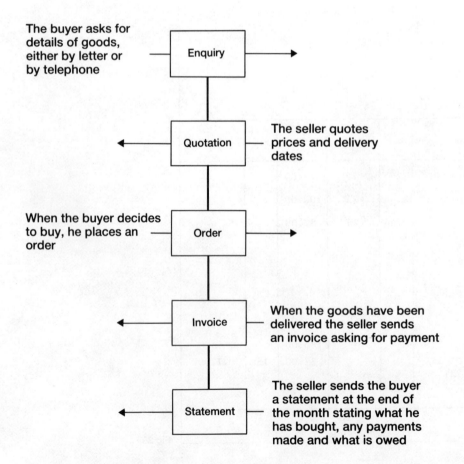

Buyer　　　　　　　　　　　　　　　　**Seller**

The buyer asks for details of goods, either by letter or by telephone — **Enquiry** →

← **Quotation** — The seller quotes prices and delivery dates

When the buyer decides to buy, he places an order — **Order** →

← **Invoice** — When the goods have been delivered the seller sends an invoice asking for payment

← **Statement** — The seller sends the buyer a statement at the end of the month stating what he has bought, any payments made and what is owed

Fig 36

4 The computer can be programmed (that is given a set of instructions) so that it will calculate prices, VAT, deduct discounts and arrive at the final total.
5 The computer will then print the invoice. This is known as the output.
6 Some computers can be programmed so that stock levels will be updated.

BAR CODES

In common with other supermarkets Bradford Superstores use bar coding for pricing at the cash desk. Each item has its own bar code. (See Fig 37.)

5 010142 284003

Fig 37

Each item is scanned over a screen at the cash desk. The data on the bar code is transmitted to the computer. The computer sends back the price which appears on a screen at the cash desk, so the customer and the cashier can see it. The item is then recorded.

In addition the computer adjusts the stock level. The computer will indicate when minimum levels have been reached and new stock needs to be ordered. Some computers may be programmed to re-order further goods automatically.

CHECK YOUR PROGRESS

1 On a cheque – who is the drawer?
                – who is the drawee?
                – who is the payee?
2 State four reasons why a cheque might be referred to drawer.
3 State four points which should be checked before accepting a cheque.
4 What is the purpose of a counterfoil on a paying-in slip?
5 What is meant by reconciling a bank statement?
6 What information is contained on a petty cash voucher?
7 What is the purpose of the imprest system?
8 What is an invoice and what information does it contain?
9 Place the following in the correct order for a simple business transaction:

    Quotation
    Invoice
    Enquiry
    Statement
    Order
10 Explain the use of bar codes.

Copy out and *tick* if you are able to:
- Check a cheque
- Complete a paying-in slip
- Understand a bank statement
- Complete a petty cash voucher
- Operate an imprest system
- Calculate expenses
- Calculate invoices
- Explain the use of bar codes
- Explain how computers may be used in preparing invoices

5   WAGES DEPARTMENT

You are now assisting in the Wages Department. The wages of full-time staff are prepared on the computer, but wages for temporary staff, ie students working in the summer vacation or at Christmas are prepared part-manually and then by computer. Your duties will be to help with the manual preparation of wages, with the exception of calculating income tax. This work will be done by the wages clerk.

You may find the following basic procedures helpful in calculating wages:

1   Calculate the gross wage (this may be hourly, weekly or monthly).
2   Add any bonus or overtime.
3   Calculate and deduct National Insurance (NI) payments using National Insurance tables.
4   Calculate and deduct income tax payments using special tax tables (this is known as PAYE – Pay As You Earn).
5   Deduct any voluntary deductions, eg union subscriptions, superannuation, holiday savings, etc.
6   This leaves the *net* wages – or, as it is commonly referred to, the 'take-home' pay.

In addition to calculating and paying wages the employer has to keep the following records:

a   Details of each employee's income tax and NI payments are kept on a separate tax card. This is known as a **P11**. Each employee has a separate card. (See Fig 38.)
b   Details of all employee's wages, including NI and income tax deducations are kept on a payroll sheet.
c   In addition, if the wages are to be paid in cash (and this is usual for temporary staff) the employer must prepare a coin analysis sheet to take to the bank in order to have the correct amount of money to make up into the wage packets.

★   **Memory joggers**

1   **What is the first step in calculating wages?**
2   **What is the gross wage?**
3   **What is the net wage?**
4   **State the two compulsory deductions.**

★   **Decisions! Decisions!**

●   **If you were offered a job at £3500, what would your basic weekly wage be? Use your calculator.**
●   **If you were offered a job at £4000 what would your monthly salary be? Differentiate between the *gross* wage and the *net* wage.**

CALCULATION OF WAGES

The way in which salaries are paid varies from company to company. Generally speaking manual workers and temporary workers are paid weekly either in cash or by cheque, whilst most other employees are paid monthly. Workers paid by calendar months earn an annual salary of which they receive one-twelfth each month.

Time rates

This is the rate of pay for each hour worked. Normally a higher rate is paid for overtime. This may be time and a half or double time.

Deductions working sheet P11 (New)

Employee's surname in CAPITAL LETTERS

Employee's name

First two forenames

Year to
5 April
19......

Tax District and reference

National Insurance no.

Date of birth
in figures
Day | Month | Year

Works no. etc.

Date of leaving
in figures
Day | Month | Year

Tax Code †

Amended
code †

Week/Month/
no. in which
applied

National Insurance Contributions *

Total of Employee's and Employer's Contributions payable 1a	Employee's contributions payable 1b	Employee's contributions at Contracted-out rate included in Col. 1b 1c	Statutory sick pay in the week or month included in col. 2 1d	MONTH number	WEEK number	Pay in the week or month including statutory sick pay 2	Total pay to date 3	Total free pay to date as shown by Table A 4	Total taxable pay to date ∅ 5	Total tax due to date as shown by Taxable Pay Tables 6	Tax deducted or refunded in the week or month Mark refunds 'R' 7	For employer's use
£	£	£	£			£	£	£	£	£	£	£
				6 April to 5 May	1							
					2							
					3							
				1	4							
				6 May to 5 June	5							
					6							
					7							
				2	8							
				6 June to 5 July	9							
					10							
					11							
					12							
				3	13							
				6 July to 5 Aug.	14							
					15							
					16							
				4	17							
				6 Aug. to 5 Sept.	18							
					19							
					20							
				5	21							
				6 Sept. to 5 Oct.	22							
					23							
					24							
					25							
				6	26							
				6 Oct. to 5 Nov.	27							
					28							
					29							
				7	30							
Total carried forward	Total carried forward	Total carried forward	Total carried forward	Total carried forward								

PAYE Income Tax

* N.I. Contribution Table letter must be entered overleaf beside the N.I. totals boxes – see the note shown there. This box may be used if the employer wishes to record the N.I. letter while this side of the sheet is in use

† If amended cross out previous code
∅ If in any week/month the amount in column 4 is more than the amount in column 3, make no entry in column 3.

P11
(New)

Fig 38

SPECIMEN

If an employee arrives late a proportion of the hourly rate would be deducted, usually calculated to the quarter hour.

Each employee has a time card – kept in a rack next to a time clock. He/she clocks in and out. The cards act as a record of attendance and also to calculate wages. The number of hours multiplied by the hourly rate equals the gross pay. Sometimes additional payments are made for a variety of reasons. These include:

Overtime   This is usually paid at a higher rate than the work carried out during normal working time.

Piece rates   These are often paid as an incentive to greater productivity. The employee is paid a certain amount for each piece of work produced. There are certain offices where work is measured, ie in a word processing or audio-typing pool, and operators are paid a bonus above their basic wage.

Commission   This method is often employed by companies employing sales representatives. They usually, although not always, receive a basic salary plus a percentage on the sales transacted.

★   **Memory joggers**

1   **Explain the various ways in which the gross pay may be calculated.**
2   **What additional payments may be added to the basic wage?**

★   **Decisions! Decisions!**

●   **What method of calculation of the gross wage might be used for the following employees:**

　　Supervisors
　　Cleaner working part time
　　Sales representative
　　Security guard working extra week-ends
　　Full-time cash till operator
　　Shelf-stacker with a set target of shelves to fill per day

Trainee task 32 (a)

Bradford Superstores employs a number of temporary part-time workers during the holiday season. Calculate the following gross wages:

Job	Hours	Rate per hour
Part-time check-out operator	15	£2.00 per hour
Saturday staff	8	£1.50 per hour under 18
Saturday staff	8	£1.75 per hour over 18
Saturday security staff	12*	£3.00 per hour – basic rate
Sunday security staff	4**	£3.00 per hour – basic rate

　* 8 hours basic rate + 4 hours time and a half
** Sunday rate to be paid at double time

★   **Memory joggers**

1   **What are the compulsory deductions from the gross wage?**
2   **What are the voluntary deductions?**

STATUTORY DEDUCTIONS

These are compulsory deductions which are deducted by the employer on behalf of the government. There are two statutory deductions – income tax and National Insurance.

Income Tax – mainly by PAYE (Pay As You Earn)

Tax tables are sent out each year to the employers giving the amount of tax to be paid, calculated on taxable pay.

Every employee is allocated a **code number** – based on personal circumstances (marital, number of dependants, allowances – life assurance premiums, etc). A claim for allowances is filled in each year to calculate allowances.

This **code number** determines the amount of tax free pay. If this is the same or more than earnings no tax if paid. A tax year runs from 6 April to 5 April.

At the end of each year, each employee receives a **P60** form. This states the total earnings and the amount of tax paid. This should be kept in a safe place as it may be needed at a future date to claim earnings-related social security benefits. (See Fig 39.)

Trainee task 33 (a)

- Find out the current rates of standard income tax. Find out how much a single person can earn before paying tax.

- From the P60 below, how much has this employee earned and how much tax has he paid?

If an employee changes his job during the tax year his/her emloyer issues in triplicate a form **P45** which states total earnings, tax paid and code number. This is given to the Wages Department of the new firm. (See Fig 40.)

SPECIMEN

P60 Certificate of pay, tax deducted and National Insurance contributions

DO NOT DESTROY

Employee's National Insurance No.	Final tax code	Employer's PAYE reference	Year to 5 April
AB 13 82 23 C	180 L	928 L2	**198**5...

Employee's surname	Forenames or initials
FERGUSON	A C

1. Previous employment				2. This employment		
Pay		Tax		Pay	Tax *(if refund mark 'R')*	
£ − −		£ − −		£ 12,762 ¦ 62	£ 3,285 ¦ 90	

National Insurance contributions in this employment		
Contribution Table Letter	Employee's contributions payable	Employee's contributions at Contracted-out rate included in previous column
E	£ 470 ¦ 52	£ − ¦ −
	£	£
	£	£
	£	£

I/we certify that the particulars given above include the total amount of pay for income tax purposes (including overtime, bonus, commission, etc.) paid to you by me/us in the year ended 5 April last, and the total tax and National Insurance contributions deducted by me/us (less any refunds) in that year.

Employer's name *(in full)* .... BRADFORD SUPERSTORES ....

Address *(in full)* .... Kings Road BRADFORD BD9 8PL ....

TO THE EMPLOYEE

Keep this certificate. It will help you to check any Notice of Assessment which the Tax Office may send you in due course. You can also use it to check that your employer is deducting the right type of National Insurance contributions for you and using your correct National Insurance number. If he is not, you should tell him. You cannot get a duplicate form P60.

P60

840916 Dd 8400949 200m 10/84 StS.

Fig 39

P45 — **Details of EMPLOYEE LEAVING** — PART 1

1. PAYE reference	District number: 928	Reference number: L2
2. National Insurance number	W E 55 12 87 A	
3. Surname (Use BLOCK letters)	CHRISTIE	Mr. Mrs. Miss: MR
First two forenames (Use BLOCK letters)	JEFFREY	
4. Date of leaving (in figures)	Day 22, Month 2	Year 19 85
5. Code at date of leaving. If Week 1 or Month 1 basis applies, please also write "X" in the box marked "Week 1 or Month 1"	Code: 320 H	Week 1 or Month 1:

6. Last entries on Deductions Working Sheet. If Week 1 or Month 1 basis applies, complete item 7 instead			
	Week or Month number	Week: 47	Month:
	Total pay to date	£ 6948	p
	Total tax to date	£ 1123	p
7. Week 1 or Month 1 basis applies	Total pay in this employment	£	p
	Total tax in this employment	£	p

8. Works Number	750	9. Branch, Contract Department, etc.	Stores

10. Employee's private address: 24 Maynard Street, BRADFORD. Postcode BD12 4NT

11. I certify that the details entered at items 1 to 9 above are correct.

Employer: BRADFORD SUPERSTORES

Address: Kings Road, BRADFORD

Date: 22 February 1985 Postcode: BD9 8PL

For Tax Office use

For Centre 1 use: Amended | M/E | P

INSTRUCTIONS TO EMPLOYER

- Complete this form according to the "Employee leaving" instructions on the P8 (BLUE CARD).
- Detach Part 1 and send it to your Tax Office IMMEDIATELY.
- Hand Parts 2 and 3 (unseparated) to your employee WHEN HE LEAVES.
- IF THE EMPLOYEE HAS DIED, please write "D" in this box and send ALL THREE PARTS of this form (unseparated) to your Tax Office IMMEDIATELY.

P45 HPB 1166 11/83

SPECIMEN

Fig 40 Part 1 sent to local tax office. Parts 2 and 3 given to employee to take to new employer.

Trainee task 34 (a)

- State the employee's total earnings.
- How much tax has he paid?
- What is his code number?

★ **Memory joggers**

1 **When does the tax year start? When does it end?**
2 **What information is contained on a P60? When is it issued?**
3 **What form is given to an employee when he changes his job?**

National Insurance

Everyone over school-leaving age is liable to pay this if employed, self-employed and in some cases unemployed. There are different classes and each pays a different rate – it is now calculated on the weekly/monthly wage.

Regular contributions entitle a person to claim benefits for sickness, unemployment or injury at work. Other benefits include a retirement pension (self or widow). Women may also receive maternity benefits.

Every employee must have a card which is obtainable from the Department of Health and Social Security. The card shows the individual's National Insurance number which must be quoted whenever claims are made.

Records of all National Insurance numbers are kept by the DHSS (Department of Health and Social Security) on computer. In April 1984 there were 51 million records on computer.

Trainee task 35 (a)

The current National Insurance rates are shown on page 46 (Fig 41).

You are required to calculate the correct employees' contributions for the following personnel:

Personnel	*Wage*
T Clough	£93.50
T Patel	£98.00
S Bedford	£128.50
J Hobson	£85.00
J Bruce	£101.00
P Walton	£143.00
M Idris	£126.50
R Parsons	£116.00
C Jinks	£133.00
B Scott	£88.00

★ **Memory joggers**

1 **What are the two compulsory deductions from wages?**
2 **What benefits might employees receive from their National Insurance contributions?**
3 **What other deductions are there from the gross wage?**

READING A PAY SLIP

A colleague has received her first wage slip and is unable to understand the various deductions. (See Fig 42.)

Trainee task 36 (a)

- Explain to her what is meant by gross pay and net pay.
- Explain the various deductions.
- Explain what extra benefit a woman may receive from her National Insurance contributions.

CREDIT TRANSFER

At one time nearly everybody received their money in cash but nowadays more and more companies are paying their staff by cheque, or alternatively by credit transfer which means that the company pays an employee's salary straight into his or her bank account.

Fig 42 Wage slip

Name	Date	Works No	Basic pay £	Over-time £	Gross pay £	NI £	Income tax £	Other deductions £	Total deductions £	NET PAY £
						Deductions				
A. JARVIS	22–27 Feb 85	132	67.69		67.69	6.05	8.71		14.76	52.93

Weekly Table A

FOR USE FROM 6 APRIL 1985 TO 5 APRIL 1986

Gross pay	Total of employee's and employer's contributions payable	Employee's contribution payable	Employer's contribution*	Gross pay	Total of employee's and employer's contributions payable	Employee's contribution payable	Employer's contribution*
£	£	£	£	£	£	£	£
85·00	16·58	7·67	8·91	115·00	22·41	10·37	12·04
85·50	16·68	7·72	8·96	115·50	22·52	10·42	12·10
86·00	16·77	7·76	9·01	116·00	22·61	10·46	12·15
86·50	16·88	7·81	9·07	116·50	22·71	10·51	12·20
87·00	16·97	7·85	9·12	117·00	22·80	10·55	12·25
87·50	17·07	7·90	9·17	117·50	22·90	10·60	12·30
88·00	17·16	7·94	9·22	118·00	23·00	10·64	12·36
88·50	17·26	7·99	9·27	118·50	23·10	10·69	12·41
89·00	17·36	8·03	9·33	119·00	23·19	10·73	12·46
89·50	17·46	8·08	9·38	119·50	23·29	10·78	12·51
90·00	17·55	8·12	9·43	120·00	23·39	10·82	12·57
90·50	17·65	8·17	9·48	120·50	23·49	10·87	12·62
91·00	17·75	8·21	9·54	121·00	23·58	10·91	12·67
91·50	17·85	8·26	9·59	121·50	23·68	10·96	12·72
92·00	17·94	8·30	9·64	122·00	23·78	11·00	12·78
92·50	18·04	8·35	9·69	122·50	23·88	11·05	12·83
93·00	18·13	8·39	9·74	123·00	23·97	11·09	12·88
93·50	18·24	8·44	9·80	123·50	24·07	11·14	12·93
94·00	18·33	8·48	9·85	124·00	24·16	11·18	12·98
94·50	18·43	8·53	9·90	124·50	24·27	11·23	13·04
95·00	18·52	8·57	9·95	125·00	24·36	11·27	13·09
95·50	18·63	8·62	10·01	125·50	24·46	11·32	13·14
96·00	18·72	8·66	10·06	126·00	24·55	11·36	13·19
96·50	18·82	8·71	10·11	126·50	24·66	11·41	13·25
97·00	18·91	8·75	10·16	127·00	24·75	11·45	13·30
97·50	19·01	8·80	10·21	127·50	24·85	11·50	13·35
98·00	19·11	8·84	10·27	128·00	24·94	11·54	13·40
98·50	19·21	8·89	10·32	128·50	25·04	11·59	13·45
99·00	19·30	8·93	10·37	129·00	25·14	11·63	13·51
99·50	19·40	8·98	10·42	129·50	25·24	11·68	13·56
100·00	19·50	9·02	10·48	130·00	25·33	11·72	13·61
100·50	19·60	9·07	10·53	130·50	25·43	11·77	13·66
101·00	19·69	9·11	10·58	131·00	25·53	11·81	13·72
101·50	19·79	9·16	10·63	131·50	25·63	11·86	13·77
102·00	19·89	9·20	10·69	132·00	25·72	11·90	13·82
102·50	19·99	9·25	10·74	132·50	25·82	11·95	13·87
103·00	20·08	9·29	10·79	133·00	25·91	11·99	13·92
103·50	20·18	9·34	10·84	133·50	26·02	12·04	13·98
104·00	20·27	9·38	10·89	134·00	26·11	12·08	14·03
104·50	20·38	9·43	10·95	134·50	26·21	12·13	14·08
105·00	20·47	9·47	11·00	135·00	26·30	12·17	14·13
105·50	20·57	9·52	11·05	135·50	26·41	12·22	14·19
106·00	20·66	9·56	11·10	136·00	26·50	12·26	14·24
106·50	20·77	9·61	11·16	136·50	26·60	12·31	14·29
107·00	20·86	9·65	11·21	137·00	26·69	12·35	14·34
107·50	20·96	9·70	11·26	137·50	26·79	12·40	14·39
108·00	21·05	9·74	11·31	138·00	26·89	12·44	14·45
108·50	21·15	9·79	11·36	138·50	26·99	12·49	14·50
109·00	21·25	9·83	11·42	139·00	27·08	12·53	14·55
109·50	21·35	9·88	11·47	139·50	27·18	12·58	14·60
110·00	21·44	9·92	11·52	140·00	27·28	12·62	14·66
110·50	21·54	9·97	11·57	140·50	27·38	12·67	14·71
111·00	21·64	10·01	11·63	141·00	27·47	12·71	14·76
111·50	21·74	10·06	11·68	141·50	27·57	12·76	14·81
112·00	21·83	10·10	11·73	142·00	27·67	12·80	14·87
112·50	21·93	10·15	11·78	142·50	27·77	12·85	14·92
113·00	22·02	10·19	11·83	143·00	27·86	12·89	14·97
113·50	22·13	10·24	11·89	143·50	27·96	12·94	15·02
114·00	22·22	10·28	11·94	144·00	28·05	12·98	15·07
114·50	22·32	10·33	11·99	144·50	28·16	13·03	15·13

* For information only. DO NOT ENTER ON DEDUCTIONS WORKING SHEET (P11 NEW).

Fig 41

★ **Decisions! Decisions!**

- **Why do you think employers prefer to pay wages by credit transfer?**
- **What are the advantages for the employer?**
- **Are there any advantages for the employee?**

Trainee task 37 (a)

Prepare a memo from the Wages Section inviting staff to have their wages paid by credit transfer. Indicate the advantages.

PAYROLL

An employer has to keep records of all earnings, deductions and contributions of his employees. Listed below is a sample of the payroll. (See Fig 43.)

Trainee task 38 (a)

- Calculate the *net pay* for each employee.
- Calculate the totals for overtime, income tax, National Insurance and *net pay*.

PAYMENT BY CASH

Although many employees are paid by credit transfer or cheque, some are still paid by cash. The employer needs to know exactly how much cash to draw from the bank in order to make up each wage packet. Therefore from the payroll, he would complete a coin analysis form. (See Fig 44.)

Trainee task 39 (a)

- Complete the remaining figures for each employee. The first line has been completed for you as an example. You have previously calculated the *net pay* for these employees in Task 38 (a).
- When you have entered all details, then total all the columns.

Many trainees are anxious to know whether they will start paying income tax immediately they commence work. The answer to this question in general terms is 'yes'. However, if you start your first job part way through the tax year, you may get a tax refund from your employer when you have claimed your allowances and your PAYE code has been sorted out.

Fig 43

Name	Basic wage	Overtime	Gross pay	Income tax	National Insurance	Total deductions	NET PAY
	£	£	£	£	£	£	£
A WHITE	80.00	18.00	98.00	14.00	8.84	22.84	75.16
D CHILDS	90.00	10.00	100.00	13.50	8.17		
A HEPTON	95.00	25.00	120.00	15.00	10.82		
W BAKER	98.00	32.00	130.00	20.05	11.81		

Name	Net pay	£20	£10	£5	£1	50p	10p	5p	2p	1p
A WHITE	£75.16	3	1	1			1	1		1
D CHILDS										
A HEPTON										
W BAKER										

Fig 44

★ Memory joggers

1 What is a PAYE code?
2 Have you managed to find out the current rates for income tax?

For your sample folders

You may find the following leaflets helpful in understanding income tax:
'Income Tax Pay As You Earn – IR 34'; *'Income Tax – Personal Allowances – IR 22'*. Both these leaflets are obtainable from your local tax office.

COMPUTERS AND THE PREPARATION OF WAGES

The calculation of wages is very suitable for computers since it involves regular record-keeping and calculations. It is often the first use which firms make of computers. Listed below is a simple example of how a computerised wage system might operate. (See Fig 45.)

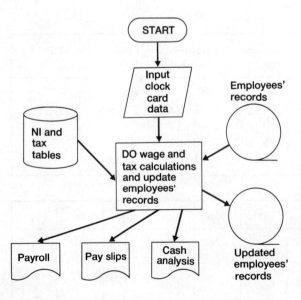

Fig 45

1 A database would be created which contains tax tables and NI rates. In addition there would be another database containing employees' records.
2 Current data from clock cards would be keyed into the computer.
3 The operator would then load a special wages program which would instruct the computer to calculate and deduct income tax and National Insurance contributions from information in the databases.
4 The computer would then calculate the net wage and at the same time would update employees' records.
5 The computer would then print out the employees' wage slips and in addition may be programmed to calculate the cash analysis.

CHECK YOUR PROGRESS

1 State the various methods of calculating the gross wage.
2 Explain two compulsory deductions from the gross wage.
3 Place the following procedures in the correct order for the calculation of wages:

> Calculation of net wage
> Calculation and deduction of National Insurance
> Calculation of gross wage
> Deduction of income tax
> Calculation of income tax
> Deduction of voluntary contributions
> Addition of bonus or overtime

4 What is the purpose of a code number?
5 What is a P60 and what items does this form contain?
6 What form is handed to an employee when he leaves a firm?
7 What additional payments might be added to the basic wage?
8 Why do firms prefer employees to be paid by the credit transfer system?
9 What form should be completed if wages are paid in cash?
10 How might a computer help in the calculation of wages?

Copy out and *tick* if you are able to:

- State the procedures for the calculation of wages
- Calculate the gross wage
- Calculate National Insurance contributions
- Calculate the net wage
- Calculate the pay roll
- Calculate a cash analysis form
- Read and explain a wage slip
- Appreciate how a computer might help in the wages transaction

6 RECEPTION

You are now working in the Reception Office. This is a very important area of any organisation as this is usually the first place where a visitor calls, therefore it is very important to create a good first impression.

The appearance and furniture of the reception area and the courtesy and efficiency of the receptionist are vital in creating this good first impression.

You may find the following hints useful in reception work:

- Be friendly and helpful
- Be courteous and polite
- Pay attention and listen to the visitor or caller
- Check appointments in the appointment book. This is a book listing all appointments for the day
- Introduce all visitors stating their name, name of their company and position within the company
- If the visitor does not have an appointment, find out the reason for their visit and who they want to see
- Discreetly find out if the person the visitor wishes to see is available and whether they will receive the visitor without an appointment
- If the caller cannot be seen without an appointment, suggest another person instead, or make a further appointment
- If the caller wishes to leave a message, write it down immediately and make sure it reaches the right person as soon as possible

★ **Memory jogger**

Why is the reception area considered a very important area of any organisation?

★ **Decisions! Decisions!**

● **What personal qualities do you think desirable for a receptionist and why? Yes, that's right:**

● **a receptionist should be well-spoken, in order to create a good first impression**
● **a receptionist should be pleasant and courteous**
● **a receptionist should be patient as they may have to deal with shy or nervous callers**
● **a receptionist should be well groomed and should maintain a high standard of hygiene**
● **a receptionist should have a sense of responsibility, eg responsibility for maintaining the tidy appearance of the reception area, responsibility for security, tactfully making certain that no unauthorised person is allowed into the building**
● **a receptionist should be tactful in dealing with casual callers without an appointment**

In addition the receptionist needs to have a good knowledge of the structure of the organisation and staff.

APPOINTMENTS BOOK

Illustrated in Fig 46 is a sample of the appointments book kept in the reception area. Each department prepares a list of appointments the day beforehand and sends a copy to the receptionist who will then know who to expect:

Date	Time	Person/Department	Name of caller
4.1	9.00	Personnel Jack Platt — Sales	D Wood B Black — Fast Foods Ltd
	9.15	General Office B Taylor — Personnel	Smiths Typewriters W Jenkins
	9.30	C Eves — Wages B Taylor — Personnel R Riles — Sales	Office Systems Ltd (J Brown) A White R Killerby — Promotions Ltd
	9.45	B Hunt — Purchasing	H Howard — Howard Printers
	10.00	B Taylor — Personnel R Riles — Sales	B Clark S Haney — York Wines Ltd
	10.15	B Taylor — Personnel General Office	E Lawler J Jackson — Brit. Telecom

Fig 46

Trainee task 40 (a)

- From the above list, state how many callers are expected for the General Office. How many callers are expected for Personnel?
- At 9.45 Miss Gray of the Leeds Staff Bureau arrives at reception wishing to speak to Mr Taylor the Personnel Officer. Is Mr Taylor free at this time?

★ **Decisions! Decisions!**

- **How will you deal with this visitor who does not have an appointment?**

★ **Memory joggers**

What are the personal qualities desirable for a receptionist? Prepare a list.

RECEPTION REGISTER

As a means of security a reception register or a visitors' book is used to record the names of all visitors, the time of arrival and who they wish to see. When the visitor leaves the time is recorded and the visitor may be asked to sign the book.

★ **Decisions! Decisions!**

- **Why do you think a reception register is used as a means of security?**
  Yes, that's right, so that there is a record of every person in the building. This discourages unauthorised visitors from entering. Also, if there were a fire, this could be used as a register to check the personnel in the building.

Trainee task 41 (a)

Make a check list of all the information needed on a reception register. Design a reception register and complete the following entries:

- at 9.00 Mr H Rowe of Jacksons Ltd called to see D Flint the Officer Manager. He left at 9.30 am
- at 9.15 Miss J Black called to see B Taylor of Personnel. She left at 9.30 am
- at 9.20 Mrs M Martin called to see her daughter H Martin on an urgent family matter. Miss Martin works in the General Office. Mrs Martin left at 9.25 am
- at 9.25 J Casey of Fast Foods Ltd called to see Jack Platt in Sales. He left at 10.00 am

★   **Decisions! Decisions!**

● **How should a receptionist deal with a caller who has arrived without an appointment and who might have to wait an hour to see the person concerned?**

COMMUNICATING BY TELEPHONE

The importance of the correct use of the telephone cannot be over estimated. As with a business letter, the efficiency of a company is often judged by the efficiency of the person who is making or receiving a telephone call.

Imagine the annoyance caused by lack of courtesy and inefficiency over the phone. Money can be wasted because of lengthy and badly-handled telephone calls.

★   **Decisions! Decisions!**

● **What points should you check before making a telephone call?**
  Yes, that's right you would check:

● **that you have the correct telephone number**
● **that you have made a note of the message you want to give**
● **that you have included all points necessary for the message**
● **that you have considered any possible queries**
● **that you have a pad and pencil by your side for taking any messages**

Receiving a call

When receiving or answering a telephone call, you may find the following procedures useful:

● Answer with the name of your company
● Ask the caller to whom he wishes to speak
● Ask the caller for his name if he has not identified himself
● Ask the caller to hold the line while you are connecting the call to an extension
● Ring the person wanted, then inform him of the caller's name
● If the call is accepted, tell the caller he is being connected
● If for any reason the call is not accepted, or

the person wanted is unavailable, offer to take a message
● Be polite and courteous at all times

Telephone calls

As a receptionist you are often required to take telephone messages. Callers often leave messages with you if the person they wish to speak to is out or unavailable. In order that you do not forget any message, you write them down to pass on to the person concerned.

★   **Decisions! Decisions!**

● **What information will you need to obtain from the caller so that you can pass on a clear message?**
  Yes, that's correct, you will need to include the following:

● **name of the caller**
● **his/her telephone number**
● **name of caller's company (and possibly the address)**
● **the message**
● **details of any action to be taken**

Trainee task 42 (a)

On an A5 sheet of paper design a telephone message sheet to include all the above items. In addition you will need to include the time of the call, the date and space for the operator's signature.

On your telephone message sheet complete details of the following telephone call:

Mr T Robinson of J R Wilson & Co (Newcastle 29631) telephoned and asks to speak to Mr Evans. You explain that Mr Evans is at a meeting and Mr Robinson decides to leave a message for him. Prepare the message and include the essential points from the following:
'A consignment is due to arrive on Thursday next and Wilsons will have a large delivery of bacon, cheese and butter. They will be in a position to supply our order on Saturday but Mr Robinson wishes to know whether the storeman will

be on duty to receive delivery. Please telephone your answer later today.'

Trainee task 43 (a)

Find out details about the following telephone services:

- ADC
- Credit card calls
- Fixed time calls
- Freefone
- Transferred charge calls
- Find out the times for Peak rates, Standard rates and Cheap rates

★ **Memory joggers**

1 **What procedures will you follow when receiving a telephone call?**
2 **What information should you obtain from the caller when taking a telephone message?**

★ **Decisions! Decisions!**

- **What would you do, as a telephonist, when connecting a call, if the extension you want is engaged?**
  Yes, that's right, you would inform the caller the extension is engaged and ask whether they will wait. If so, keep in contact with them at frequent intervals. If the delay is likely to be a long time, offer to call them back.

USE OF TELEPHONE DIRECTORIES

A good receptionist must be able to use telephone directories/The Phone Book efficiently and quickly. Many callers at the reception office ask the receptionist for local information, eg times of trains, the nearest bus stop, etc.

Trainee task 44 (a)

Using your local telephone directory/Phone Book, find the telephone numbers for the following local services:

Bus station
Coach station
Rail station
Airport
Hospital
Council offices
Job Centre
Motor Taxation Department
Gas – emergency number
Electricity
Police station
AA
RAC
Radio station
University
College of Further Education

YELLOW PAGES

Yellow Pages is a directory of business addresses and telephone numbers compiled by British Telecom. The businesses are classified in alphabetical order.

Using your local *Yellow Pages* find out the names, addresses and telephone numbers of the nearest:

Car hire service
Industrial photographer
Three hotels
Three guest houses
Car break-down recovery service

TRAVEL TIMETABLES

Miss Ann Sedivy is coming for an interview at the Leeds stores on Monday next. She is travelling from Manchester to Leeds. Her interview is at 11.15 am.

She has telephoned Head Office to ask the location of the Leeds store (it is 5 minutes from the station) and whether you could tell her the times of the trains.

Mondays to Saturdays continued

Second Class Only unless otherwise shown

		♣		♣		♣	SX	SO		♣	BHX		BHX
Leeds	d.	1325	1350	1425	1450		1525	1550	1550		1625	1630	1650	1713
Morley	d.		1400		1500			1600	1600			1640	1701	1723
Batley	d.		1405		1505			1605	1605			1645	1706	1728
Dewsbury	d.	1340	1408	1440	1508		1540	1608	1608		1640	1648	1709	1731
Ravensthorpe	d.		1411		1511			1611	1611			1651	1712	1734
Wakefield Westgate	d.					1510				1616				
Wakefield Kirkgate	d.					1516				1623				
Mirfield	d.		1415		1515	1528		1614	1614	1635		1655	1715	1737
Deighton■	d.		1420		1520	1534		1619	1619	1640		1700	1720	1742
Huddersfield	a.	1351	1425	1451	1525	1539	1551	1624	1624	1645	1651	1705	1725	1747
Huddersfield	d.	1352		1452	1526		1552		1625		1652	1706	1727	1800
Slaithwaite■	a.				1535				1633			1715	1735	1809
Marsden■	a.				1541				1639			1721	1741	1815
Greenfield	a.								1647					1823
Mossley	a.								1651					1827
Stalybridge	a.	1416		1516			1616		1656		1716			1832
Ashton-under-Lyne	a.								1700					1837
Park	a.								1706					
Miles Platting	a.								1708					
Manchester Victoria	a.	1431		1531			1631		1714		1731			1845

		SO	♣A	SX	♣	SX	SO		♣			♣		
Manchester Victoria	d.		0840		0852	0908			0952			1052		
Miles Platting	d.													
Park	d.													
Ashton-under-Lyne	d.					0919								
Stalybridge	d.		0854		0906	0924	0924		1006			1104		
Mossley	d.					0929	0929							
Greenfield	d.					0934	0934							
Marsden■	d.					0943	0943						1150	
Slaithwaite■	d.					0948	0948						1154	
Huddersfield	a.		0917		0927	0954	0954		1027			1127	1201	
Huddersfield	d.	0912	0919	0920	0928	0957	0957	1021	1028	1103	1115	1128	1203	1215
Deighton■	d.	0916		0924		1001	1001	1025		1107	1119		1207	1219
Mirfield	d.	0921		0929		1006	1006	1030		1112	1124		1212	1224
Wakefield Kirkgate	a.	0933		0941				1042			1136			1236
Wakefield Westgate	a.	0945		0954				1051			1143			1246
Ravensthorpe	d.					1010	1010			1116			1216	
Dewsbury	d.		0940			1014	1014		1040	1120		1140	1220	
Batley	d.					1017	1017			1123			1223	
Morley	d.					1023	1023			1129			1229	
Leeds	a.		0946	0957		1032	1032		1057	1139		1157	1239	

Notes: **a** Arrive. **c** Arrives 0851 on Saturdays 26 May to 8 September. **d** Depart.
A Saturdays 26 May to 8 September only. **MX** Mondays excepted.
SO Saturdays only. **SX** Saturdays excepted.
BHX Will not run on Bank Holidays 28 May, 27 August 1984, 1 January, 8 April and 6 May 1985.
♣ First and Second Class accommodation. ■ No staff in attendance.
The information shown is subject to alteration, especially during Public Holidays.
Please check carefully before travelling.

Fig 47

Trainee task 45 (a)

From the timetable illustrated in Fig 47 you are required to:

a Select the train which would be most convenient for Miss Sedivy to arrive in time for her interview. What time will it arrive in Leeds?

b What are the times of the return trains from Leeds and what time will they arrive in Manchester?

NEW TECHNOLOGY AND THE RECEPTIONIST

Prestel is a service which is offered by British Telecom. It is all about information. Information on just about everything you want to know, need to know or would like to know.

The way Prestel gets all this information to you is simplicity itself. All that is needed is a telephone and a television. The television will need to be specially equipped to receive Prestel. To operate Prestel and locate information, the user is provided with a small key pad (a bit like a calculator). The user merely has to press a few buttons to locate the information he requires.

There are already more than 150 organisations providing information to the Prestel computer.

Between them they have booked over 180 000 Prestel pages. The system will be quite capable of providing over one million separate pages of information in the future. All information on Prestel is regularly up-dated, so the user is sure that the information is up to date.

The receptionist might use Prestel to find out information on :

Air travel
Rail travel
Travel agents
Car hire
Car insurance
Hotels and restaurants
Tourism
Health and safety
Job centres
Labour market
Libraries
Local news

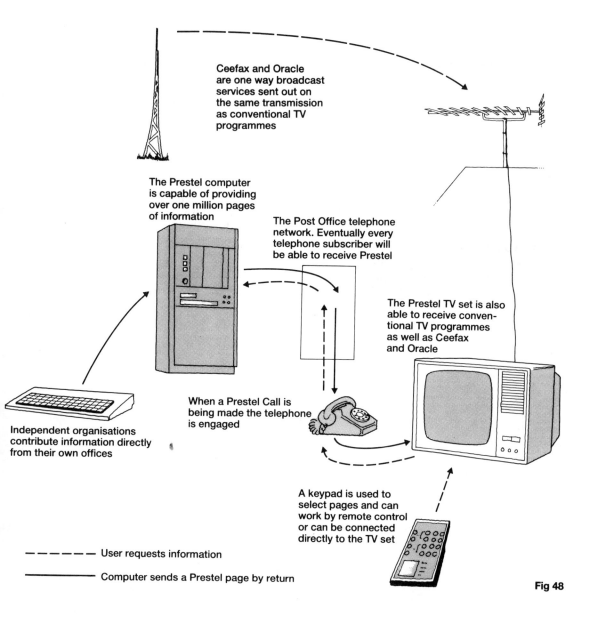

Ceefax and Oracle are one way broadcast services sent out on the same transmission as conventional TV programmes

The Prestel computer is capable of providing over one million pages of information

The Post Office telephone network. Eventually every telephone subscriber will be able to receive Prestel

The Prestel TV set is also able to receive conventional TV programmes as well as Ceefax and Oracle

Independent organisations contribute information directly from their own offices

When a Prestel Call is being made the telephone is engaged

A keypad is used to select pages and can work by remote control or can be connected directly to the TV set

— — — — — User requests information

———————— Computer sends a Prestel page by return

Fig 48

London events
Maps
Motorail
British telecommunications
Radio
Sea Link
Stock Exchange
Yellow Pages

How Prestel works is illustrated in Figure 48.

★ **Memory joggers**

1 **What equipment is needed to be able to receive Prestel?**
2 **What is used to call Prestel on the TV screen?**
3 **What information might it provide for the receptionist?**

CHECK YOUR PROGRESS

1 Why is the reception office considered to be a very important area of any organisation?
2 Outline the procedures for dealing with a caller at reception who has an appointment.
3 How would you deal with a caller who does not have an appointment?
4 Differentiate between an appointments book and a reception register.

5 Why is a reception register used as a means of security?
6 Make a list of points to check before you make a telephone call.
7 Outline the procedures for receiving a call.
8 What information would you find in the *Yellow Pages*?
9 For what purposes might a receptionist use Prestel?
10 List the duties of a trainee in the reception office.

Copy out and *tick* if you are able to:

● Explain the procedures for dealing with visitors at the reception area
● Keep an appointments register
● Keep a reception register
● Make a telephone call
● Design a simple form to take a telephone message
● Record a telephone message correctly
● Use a telephone directory/The Phone Book quickly and efficiently
● Use *Yellow Pages* quickly and efficiently
● Read and present information from a train timetable
● Appreciate the uses of Prestel

7 PERSONNEL

You are now working in the Personnel Department. The work of this department is concerned with all the staff who work for the firm. The work in Personnel will vary according to the type of organisation.

In Bradford Superstores the Personnel Department deals with the following:

- hiring new staff
- resignations, retirements and redundancy
- promotion
- staff welfare
- health and safety
- staff training
- trade unions
- wage scales
- holidays

You will be required to deal with the clerical and administrative work of these various sections of Personnel.

VACANCIES

The Personnel Department is notified when a vacancy occurs in any department.The Personnel then advertises and recruits new staff. Staff can be recruited by:

- advertising internally within the firm
- advertising in the local or national Press
- notifying job centre of vacancy
- using the services of a private employment agency

A vacancy has arisen within the Personnel Department for a records clerk. Please see Fig 49 on page 58 for a job description of the job.

Trainee task 46 (a)

From the job description in Fig 49 you are required to prepare an advertisement to be inserted in the local Press.

★ **Memory joggers**

Name three other methods of recruiting staff.

★ **Decisions! Decisions!**

- **What are the advantages to advertising a vacancy internally or notifying the job centre?**

APPLICATIONS

Some firms use an application form which they send to applicants for completion. Other firms prefer individual applications in handwriting.

Bradford Superstores has a standard letter which it uses to acknowledge applicants and to send out application forms. When the same letter concerning standard situations, eg acknowledgement of applications, needs to be sent to a number of applicants a standard letter is used. The typist merely types in the individual details. (See Fig 50 on page 59.)

Trainee task 47 (a)

You are required to send the standard letter in Fig 50 to the following applicants. This letter may be typed, but better still, if you have a word processor, this letter may be keyed in, stored and recalled as required.

JOB DESCRIPTION

Title: `Personnel Records Clerk`

Location: `Personnel Department`

Hours of work: `9.00 am - 5.00 pm Monday to Friday`

Responsible to: `Personnel Officer`

Salary: `£4029 to £4750`

Summary of Duties: `Maintain files and records for monthly, weekly, and hourly paid staff.`

`Prepare documents for all new employees.`

`Send out notification of increases in rates of pay to Heads of Departments for all employees.`

`Prepare details of vacancies for job advertisement.`

`Assist with quarterly returns for the Department of Employment`

`Prepare and maintain holiday rota in liaison with Personnel Officer.`

`Keep wage rates up-to-date.`

`Issue new rate lists where appropriate to computer controller.`

Fig 49 A job description

Name and address	Post	Closing date
Mrs S Varma 14 Armley Road BRADFORD BD29 4YJ	Typist	20 February
Mrs R Haslingden 21 Lylworth Avenue BRADFORD BD6 7TH	VDU operator	21 Febuary
Mrs S Philips 14 Elland Way BRADFORD BD10 9YT	Sales Assistant	20 February

★ **Memory jogger**

What information is contained on a job description?

★ **Decisions! Decisions!**

● **What is the purpose of sending a job description with an application form?**

Trainee task 48 (a)

Prepare a standard letter which could be sent to applicants asking them to attend for interview. Ask them to confirm whether or not they will be coming.

```
Date


Name
and
address

Dear

(Post)

Thank you for your enquiry regarding the above post. I have
pleasure in enclosing a copy of the Job Description and an
application form as requested. You will note that the
closing date is

On receipt of a completed application form an acknowledgement
will not be issued. We will write to you following the
closing date advising whether you will be called for
interview or to the effect that your application has been
unsuccessful.

Yours sincerely



PERSONNEL OFFICER

Enc
```

Fig 50

INTERVIEWS

The purposes of an interview are to:

1 Assess the applicant's suitability for the job.
2 Assess the applicant's personality.
3 Check the information given by the applicant on the application form.
4 Give the applicant information of the job.
5 Select the most suitable applicant for the job.

★ **Decisions! Decisions!**

● **Why is it necessary to consider the applicant's personality?**

REFERENCES

Employers often require references from previous employers of the applicant.

★ **Decisions! Decisions!**

● **What information might be required from a previous employer?**
  Yes, that's right:

● **whether the applicant's work was satisfactory**
● **what type of work the applicant did**
● **how long the applicant had been working for that organisation**
● **the skills and ability of the applicant**
● **personal strengths and any weaknesses of the applicant**

★ Memory joggers

1   List the main purposes of an interview.
2   What is a standard letter?

Bradford Superstores has a standard letter asking for a reference which is sent to previous employers. (See Fig 51.)

If you have access to a computer or a word processor, key in this letter to store and recall for further use.

Trainee task 49 (a)

A Miss Joanna Pasternak is to be interviewed for the post of typist in the General Office.

You are required to write to her present employer asking for a reference, using the standard letter in Fig 51. Her employer is John Langley Ltd, Dewsbury Lane, Bradford BD9 7PK.

NEW TECHNOLOGY AND THE PERSONNEL DEPARTMENT

Bradford Superstores are using word processors and computers increasingly to keep records and for their correspondence.

Illustrated in Fig 52 is a range of standard paragraphs which are stored on the computer. These paragraphs are recalled in a specific

Fig 51

```
Date


Name
and
address

Dear

Re

The above named person has applied for a vacancy with our
company and I should be most grateful for your critical
comments on her suitability for the post. Your comments
on her professional skills and personal characteristics
would also be appreciated.

I am enclosing a Job Description from which you may
judge the range of duties and responsibilities.

In order to cut down on postage we will not acknowledge
your reply but would like to take this opportunity of
thanking you in advance for your help.

Yours sincerely



PERSONNEL OFFICER

Enc
```

order to make up a document. The typist only types in the code (in this case the number) and does not retype the paragraph.

Trainee task 50 (a)

You are required to use standard paragraphs to cover the following situations:

- A letter in reply to a general enquiry about vacancies. There are none available at the moment.
- A tactful letter to an unsuccessful applicant.
- A letter calling an applicant for interview.

Use the paragraphs from Fig 52. State which paragraphs are most suitable.

Trainee task 51 (a)

- Explain what is meant by job description and by 'short list'.
- From the standard paragraphs below draft a tactful letter telling an applicant she has not reached the short list.

★ **Decisions! Decisions!**

- **What information might be contained in a letter of appointment to successful applicants?**
Yes, that's right, the offer of the post, the salary, the starting date and possibly other conditions of service.

Fig 52

---

1 Thank you for your letter of application.

2 Thank you for your recent application in connection with our vacancy.

3 Thank you for your letter in which you make enquiries about vacancies with this company.

4 I regret to advise you that following the response to recent advertising no further applications are being considered at this time.

5 I enclose an application which you should complete and return as soon as possible.

6 I enclose a Job Description for your information and attention.

7 I regret to inform you that on this occasion you have been unsuccessful.

8 Evidence of your educational qualifications will be required at your interview. In all cases photocopies are not acceptable.

9 Your application will be kept on file and I will contact you again should the situation change.

10 It has been a very difficult decision for us as the standard of applicant has been so high.

11 Unfortunately there are no suitable vacancies for which you could be considered at the present time.

12 I am sorry to inform you that your name does not appear on the short list for the second interview.

13 The response to our advertisement has been such that we are unable to interview all applicants. I regret to inform you that on this occasion you have not been successful in reaching the short list.

14 Thank you for your interest in our company and may I wish you luck in your search for suitable employment.

15 I would now like to meet you to discuss this post and suggest you telephone me to arrange a convenient date and time for an appointment for interview.

16 I apologise for the delay in writing. We are considering all applicants and will contact you again in the near future.

If the applicant wishes to take up the offer he/she writes a letter accepting the post and the conditions contained therein. This is the confirmation letter from the applicant.

FLOW CHART FOR INTERVIEWS

Below (Fig 53) is a chart illustrating the procedures to be followed from the notification of a job vacancy to the appointment of new staff.

★ **Memory jogger**

What other work is carried out in the Personnel Department besides hiring staff?

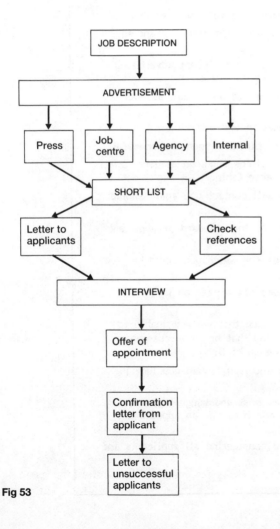

Fig 53

ABSENCES

When staff are absent due to sickness, they are required to send in a medical certificate to the Personnel Office. The Personnel Office enters all details on the employee's **record card**. This is an individual card used for each employee to record personal data and also to list absences and sick leave.

You have received a self-certification statement from Mary Crowley who works in the Accounts Department. (See Fig 54.)

Trainee task 52 (a)

You are required to find out the following information from the certificate shown in Fig 54:

a When was the first day of sickness?
b When does she expect to return to work?
c How many working days will she be absent? (She normally works a 5-day week.)

Write a memo to Ms James, Head of the Accounts Department, informing her of the situation and state when Ms Crowley is expected to return to work.

ACCIDENTS AT WORK

In 1974 The Health and Safety at Work Act was passed. This Act is concerned with employers' responsibilities for the health, safety and welfare of their employees. However the employee has certain responsibilities also. Under the terms of the Act:

1   An employee should take reasonable care to avoid injury to him/herself or to others by work activities.
2   An employee should cooperate with the employer in meeting statutory requirements.
3   An employee should not interfere with or misuse anything provided to protect his/her health, safety or welfare in compliance with the Act.

★ **Decisions! Decisions!**

• **Although office staff are less at risk from accidents with machinery than factory**

```
┌─────────────────────────────────────────────────────────────────┐
│                                                                   │
│    SELF-CERTIFICATION STATEMENT BY EMPLOYEE                        │
│        (To be completed for ALL absences where a doctor's         │
│         statement is not produced to explain the absence.)        │
│                                                                   │
│  Please complete the following statement and sign only after reading the declaration carefully: │
│  Employee's Name ____MARY  CROWLEY_____               │
│  Branch Name ____BRADFORD_____    Number __950__               │
│  Employee Number __374___    Job Title ___Accounts clerk____      │
│                                                                   │
│                       STATEMENT                                   │
│  I have been absent from work since _____18  February___(date)   │
│  and expect to return/returned (delete as appropriate) on __Monday____ │
│  ___25 February___(date) at __9.00__ am/pm.                       │
│  Was your absence as a result of your personal sickness/injury? _____YES/NO │
│  Please state briefly the specific nature of your complaint __Influenza__ │
│  _____                 │
│  _____                 │
│                                                                   │
│  If your absence was not as a result of your personal sickness/injury please state briefly the │
│  specific reason for your absence _____       │
│  _____                 │
│  _____                 │
│                                                                   │
│  Did you have permission IN ADVANCE to be absent for this reason? __NO__ YES/NO │
│                                                                   │
│                      DECLARATION                                  │
│  If I otherwise qualify to receive Sick Pay for the period of absence, please accept this personal │
│  statement as the reason for my absence and provide a Sick Pay Claim Form urgently. I declare │
│  that to the best of my knowledge and belief the information given is true and complete. │
│  I accept that the issue to me of a Sick Pay Claim Form does not constitute any liability on the │
│  part of the Company to make any payment whatsoever. I realise that knowingly and │
│  fraudulently to give false information will result in summary dismissal from the Company. │
│                                                                   │
│  Date __20/2/____    Employee's Signature __M.Crowley__           │
│                      Manager's Signature __J.Smith__              │
└─────────────────────────────────────────────────────────────────┘
```

Fig 54

staff, there are other hazards which might exist. Can you identify these?
Yes, that's right, two of the major hazards are fire and electrical appliances.

Trainee task 53 (a)

You are asked by the Safety Officer to list potential hazards which might exist in the office. You are asked for your suggestions on precautions to be taken to avoid accidents.

You are required to prepare a list identifying these dangers with precautions to be taken. Include in your list, fire hazards, electrical hazards and safety hazards. Design a poster to encourage health and safety at work and to prevent dangerous practices.

★ **Memory joggers**

State three responsibilities of the employee under the Health and Safety at Work Act.

SALARY SCALES

As a result of negotiations with the Staff Association, the management and the trade unions, it has been agreed that staff salaries will be increased by 5%. Listed below are the present salary scales:

Salary scales

Cler A	Cler B	Sec A	Sec B	PA
£	£	£	£	£
3355	4029	4575	6278	6600
3580	4267	4848	6692	7100
3808	4516	5115	7100	7600
4029	4750	5379	7502	8000

Additional increments
£500 pa for RSA III Typing
£500 pa for RSA 120 wpm shorthand
£500 pa for RSA Bilingual Secretary's Diploma

Trainee task 54 (a)

You are required to retype this list indicating the new salary scales. Increments are also to be increased by 5%. Use your calculator.

CHECK YOUR PROGRESS

1 List the work of the Personnel Department.
2 What information is contained on a job description?
3 List the purposes of an interview.
4 How might word processors and computers help in Personnel work?
5 State three responsibilities of the employee under the Health and Safety at Work Act 1974.
6 Explain four methods which might be used to recruit staff.
7 Why do companies keep staff records?
8 List the following procedures for interviewing in the correct order:

   Job description
   Short list
   Interview
   Advertisement
   Letter to unsuccessful applicants
   Offer of appointment
9 Identify three hazards concerning health and safety in the office.
10 List the duties of a clerk in the Personnel Office.

Copy out and *tick* if you are able to:

● List the duties of a clerk in the Personnel Office
● Prepare a job advertisement
● Use standard letters and standard paragraphs
● Read and understand information from a medical certificate
● Identify health and safety hazards in the office
● Up-date salary scales

8 PURCHASING

You are now working in the Purchasing Department. This department deals with all goods, services and supplies which are bought by the firm. This is often known as the Buying Department.

The types of goods and services which Bradford Superstores buy are:

- Goods and supplies bought ready for re-sale. These will be groceries, fresh food, DIY equipment and petrol.
- Goods and services used in the day-to-day running of the firm, eg stationery, cleaning and maintenance supplies.
- Goods and equipment used in the running of the firm on a permanent basis, eg typewriters, office equipment, motor vehicles.

The work of the Purchase Office is concerned with ordering goods and services, obtaining supplies, receiving the goods and storing the goods for use or resale.

★ **Memory joggers**

1 **What type of goods or services might a Purchasing Department deal with?**
2 **What type of work is done in a Purchasing Office?**

★ **Decisions! Decisions!**

- **In order to buy goods or services, it is necessary to be aware of the range of goods offered and the prices. How might a buyer obtain details and prices of goods.**
  Yes, that's right, they could consult or telephone a supplier or use a catalogue or a price list.

PRICE LISTS

Listed below is an extract from a price list:

Cat No.	Item	Price
1001	Printer RM 80 matrix dot	£219.00
1002	Printer RM 80 F/T matrix dot	£259.00
1003	Printer BM 80 matrix dot	£349.00
1004	Printer BM 100 matrix dot	£549.00
1005	Printer RX 100 daisy wheel	£400.00
1006	Saki daisy wheel printer	£399.00
1007	Printer cable (1 metre)	£11.00
1008	Printer cable (1.5 metres)	£13.00
1009	Printer Japonica daisy wheel	£450.00
1010	Japonica colour printer	£500.00
1011	Wannet daisy wheel printer	£660.00

Trainee task 55 (a)

- What information is contained on a price list?
- List the range of printers using a daisy wheel. Which is the cheapest? Which is the most expensive?
- How much would 3 metres of printer cable cost?

LETTER OF ENQUIRY

In order to find out about goods or supplies the buyer might write to the seller asking for details. This is known as a **letter of enquiry**.

★ **Decisions! Decisions!**

- **What other information might the buyer require besides price details?**
  Yes, that's right, they might like to know about the quality of the goods, the range of goods offered, details of delivery, that is how soon they would receive the goods, also whether a discount is available.

Trainee task 56 (a)

Bradford Superstores is considering buying some new electronic typewriters. They want typewriters which have a memory store, correcting facilities and daisy wheel printing.

You are required to draft a letter of enquiry to be sent to suppliers asking them to quote prices, delivery dates and whether any discount is allowed.

★ **Decisions! Decisions!**

● **Which reference book might you use to locate a list of suppliers of office equipment?**

FORM LETTERS

Instead of sending an individual letter of enquiry, often a **form letter** is used. This is a pre-printed letter which is used to elicit the same information from a number of suppliers. The individual details to each supplier, eg name and address, is the only typing required.

Forms are a quick and convenient way of collecting information. Once the form has been designed, it can be used over and over again. Everyone is asked the same questions in the same order, so that when the information is returned it is easy to collate and compare prices, terms, delivery, etc.

How forms might be used in a Purchasing Department

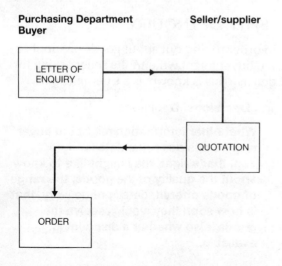

Purchasing Department   Seller/supplier
Buyer

LETTER OF ENQUIRY

QUOTATION

ORDER

★ **Memory joggers**

1 **What information might be contained in a letter of enquiry?**
2 **What is a form letter?**
3 **What are the advantages in using a form letter?**

QUOTATION

When the supplier or seller receives the letter of enquiry he/she replies quoting full particulars of the goods offered for sale including prices, terms and delivery dates. This is known as a **quotation**. Again a form letter could be used for this purpose. Fig 55 is a sample quotation.

When the quotation is received, the buyer or Purchasing Officer will have to decide which company offers the best deal.

★ **Decisions! Decisions!**

● **What factors besides price might a buyer consider in choosing a supplier? Yes, he/she would consider:**

● **the quality of the goods**
● **how much discount is allowed**
● **the delivery date**
● **whether delivery charges are included or extra**
● **whether prices include VAT**
● **after sales service**
● **maintenance if applicable**

DISCOUNTS

There are two types of discount

a Trade discount
b Cash discount

Trade discount

This is an allowance granted by the seller to the buyer. It may be an allowance given for a large order, or as a trade allowance, or as an agent's profit. It is deducted from the total amount *before* the addition of VAT.

Thank you for your recent enquiry. We have pleasure in quoting as follows:

To supply and fit drawers and shelves as per sketch — shelves only	£827.75
Using Mahogany Drawers	£1,022.75
Using Plastic Drawers	£977.75

VAT 15% to be added to all prices

Delivery 2 months after receipt of order

Terms — 10% discount for payment within 1 month

We look forward to hearing from you in due course

Fig 55

Cash discount

This is an allowance granted by the seller to the buyer to encourage prompt payment of bills. For example, 'Terms – 5% cash in one month' means that the buyer may deduct 5% from the amount due, if he/she makes payment within a month. This cash discount is often in addition to the trade discount.

★ Memory joggers

1 What other factors might influence a buyer in choosing a supplier?
2 What is the difference between trade and cash discount?

VAT

This is a trading tax which was introduced in 1973 when Britain joined the European Economic Community (EEC) or Common Market. When a firm supplies goods or services on which VAT is chargeable, they issue a 'tax invoice' showing the cost plus the VAT charged. Therefore it is the buyer who pays the VAT.

★ Decisions! Decisions!

- **What is the current rate of VAT? Is it:**
- **10% = ?**

- **15% = ?**
- **20% = ?**
- **40% = ?**

The General Office has requested some new office filing cabinets (four-drawer type). The Purchasing Office has received quotations from three firms. As part of your training programme you have been asked to select the supplier offering the best terms. The filing cabinets are of the same quality.

Trainee task 57 (a)

Listed on page 68 are three quotations. Select the supplier offering the most favourable terms.

★ Memory joggers

In choosing a quotation what other factors did you consider besides price?

PROMPT PAYMENTS

Once a week invoices which offer a cash discount for prompt payment are passed to you to be quickly processed. You are required to calculate the cash discount and enter this on the invoice. This will then be deducted from the invoice.

QUOTATION No 1

2 drawer filing cabinet
28 × 18 x 24 complete with 100 files   £91.00

4 drawer filing cabinet
51¾ x 18 x 24½ complete with 200 files   £127.00

All prices include VAT (15%)

Immediate delivery: carriage paid
10% trade discount.

QUOTATION No 2

3 drawer filing cabinet 40 x 18 x 24½   £107.00

4 drawer filing cabinet 54 x 18 x 24½   £130.00

Manilla files for cabinets — £5 per 100

All prices exclusive of VAT (15%)
Delivery — 1 month

Delivery and carriage extra
10% trade discount

QUOTATION No 3

2 drawer filing cabinet 24 x 16 x 24   £80.00

3 drawer filing cabinet 40 x 16 x 24   £100.00

4 drawer filing cabinet 54 x 16 x 24   £120.00
50 manilla files supplied with each cabinet

All prices include VAT (15%)

Delivery — 4 weeks — carriage paid
20% trade discount
  5% cash discount for settlement within 7 days

Trainee task 58 (a)

You have received the following invoices against purchase orders showing the total amount to be paid and the cash discount terms. You are required to calculate for each invoice how much the cash discount will be.

★ **Decisions! Decisions!**

● **What are the advantages of cash discount:**
● **to the buyer?**
● **to the seller?**

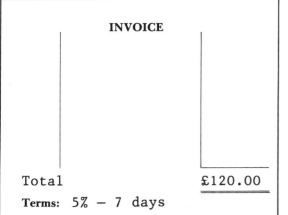

INVOICE

Total   £120.00

Terms: 5% − 7 days

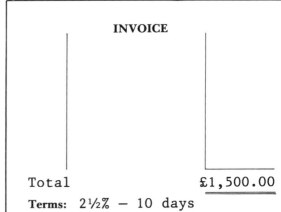

INVOICE

Total   £1,500.00

Terms: 2½% − 10 days

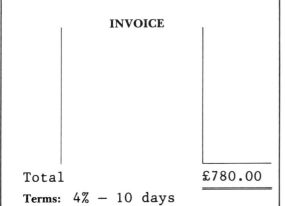

INVOICE

Total   £780.00

Terms: 4% − 10 days

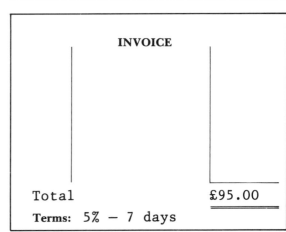

INVOICE

Total   £95.00

Terms: 5% − 7 days

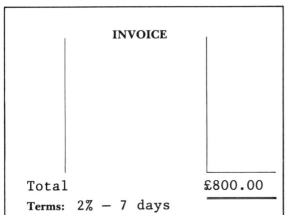

INVOICE

Total   £800.00

Terms: 2% − 7 days

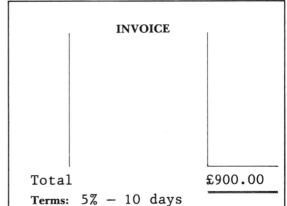

INVOICE

Total   £900.00

Terms: 5% − 10 days

ORDER

From: BRADFORD SUPERSTORES   No 248
       Kings Road
       BRADFORD   BD9 8PL
Tel: BRAD 23456   Telex: 55261 BRADSTORES

                                          Date: 20 February 19..

To: ┌─────────────────────────────┐
     │ Computer People Ltd   │
     │ Southwood House   │
     │ North Street   │
     │ HALIFAX   HA2 3BK   │
     └─────────────────────────────┘

Please supply:

Quantity	Description	Your Cat No	Price each £
200	A4 PVC Folders — green	2113	£10.90 per 100
500	A4 PVC Folders — clear	2114	£12.00 per 100

Deliver by:

    to:

                             ....
                                Buyer

Fig 56

ORDERS

When the buyer decides to buy goods or services he/she places an **order**. The original order form is sent to the supplier.

Copies of the order are sent to the departments responsible for receiving and checking the goods so that when the goods are delivered they may be checked against the order. One copy would be sent to the department which ordered the goods. Another copy would be sent to the Accounts Department for eventual payment. A further copy would be kept in the Purchasing Office.

★ **Decisions! Decisions!**

● **Why is it necessary to have copies of the original orders?**
● **Which departments might receive a copy and for what purposes?**

Illustrated opposite (Fig 56) is an order placed with a supplier for some office equipment.

Trainee task 59 (a)

From the order illustrated in Fig 56 you are required to identify the following:

● Who is the buyer?
● Who is the seller?
● When was the order sent out?
● What goods were ordered?
● What were the prices of the goods?
● What would be the total value of the order, if the supplier could supply all the goods?

★ **Decisions! Decisions!**

● **Where might the buyer obtain a description and price of the goods?**
  Yes, that's right, from the price list or catalogue
● **Why do you think the total value or cost is generally not stated on an order?**
  Yes, there may be several reasons for this. The supplier may not be able to supply all the goods at once. The prices may change, or there may be a change in VAT rate between placing the order and selling

the goods. Therefore the total price is normally shown on the invoice, or bill, when the goods are delivered.

★ **Memory joggers**

1 **What information is contained on an order?**
2 **Which departments might receive a copy of the order?**

ADVICE NOTE

When the goods are ready to send, the supplier sends an **advice note**. This is to inform the buyer when the goods are being despatched and the method of transport used. The buyer may then expect delivery and make arrangements to receive the goods.

However if the goods are to be delivered almost immediately on receipt of the order it is not necessary to send an advice note.

GOODS RECEIVED NOTE

When goods are received they need to be checked against the original order. The checker will enter details on a **goods received note** and will send a copy to the Purchasing Office. There it will be checked against the original order and if correct it will be passed for payment.

Trainee task 60 (a)

Illustrated overleaf is a goods received note. This refers to the order placed in Task 59 (a). You are required to state the following:

● How many items have been delivered?
● Who received the goods? Who checked them?

Check the delivery note against the original order. You will notice that there is a discrepancy. Write to the supplier pointing out the error and ask when you may expect a further delivery.

GOODS RECEIVED NOTE No 45

Supplier: Computer People Ltd

Date Received: 28/2/8—

Delivery/Advice Note No.:

Received per: Carrier — BRS

Order No.	Description	Quantity Received
248	A4 PVC Folders — clear	200
248	A4 PVC Folders — green	200

Received by	Date	Entered in Stock by	Date
J Brad	28-2-85		

Inspected by	B Stones	Date	28/2/85

Shortages/
Damage recorded: Satisfactory

★ **Memory joggers**

1 **What is the purpose of an advice note?**
2 **What is the purpose of a goods received note?**

In order to offer a wide range of goods to their customers the buyers at Bradford Superstores often have to travel abroad to see suppliers. They visit mainly USA, Japan, Hong Kong, France and Germany.

Trainee task 61 (a)

Using the current rates of exchange which may be obtained from banks or are often published in the newspapers, or are available via Prestel, you are required to prepare a table (like the one below) on a postcard listing the various rates for the different countries. Use your calculator.

CHECK YOUR PROGRESS

1 The Purchasing Department deals with all the goods and services which are .... by the firm.
2 List three types of goods or services which a firm might buy.

3 How might a buyer obtain details and prices of goods?
4 What are form letters and how might they be used in a Purchasing Department?
5 What is a quotation?
6 What factors might a buyer consider when choosing a supplier?
7 Differentiate between trade and cash discount.
8 What is the purpose of a goods received note?
9 What information is contained on an order?
10 List the duties of a clerk in the Purchasing Office.

Copy out and *tick* if you are able to:

● Read and understand a price list
● Quote prices when asked
● Prepare a letter of enquiry
● Read and understand a quotation
● Select the best quotation from several suppliers
● Calculate cash discount
● Check orders and goods received notes
● Convert foreign currency

Country	Currency	Rate	£1	£5	£10	£50	£100
France	Franc	10.95	10.95	54.75	109.50	547.50	1095.00
Germany							
Hong Kong							
Japan							
USA							

9 SALES

You are now working in the Sales Department. This department is concerned with the selling of goods and services. Bradford Superstores is mainly concerned with selling foods and goods in their supermarkets. They sell direct, over the counter, and payment is made by cash, cheque or credit card. However, there are clerical/administrative duties concerned with sales, eg sales figures, statistics, publicity and promotions.

However Bradford Superstores do provide services to other companies. One of these services is the selling of advertising space. Companies rent space in the stores in order to advertise their goods. These are mainly companies specialising in home improvements, double-glazing, kitchen equipment, etc.

A company introducing a new product, eg cosmetics or a new food line would possibly be interested in renting space in a prime position in order to promote, advertise or sell their goods.

There is a rental charge for this space and this varies from store to store. After the period of hire a bill or an **invoice** is sent to the customer.

Illustrated opposite (Fig 57) is an invoice sent to a company for hire of rental space.

Trainee task 62 (a)

You are required to:

- Identify who is the seller or supplier of goods/services.
- State what service has been provided.
- Who is the buyer?
- How much is the hire rent per week?
- What is the total cost?

★ **Memory joggers**

1 What information is contained on an invoice?
2 How does an invoice differ from an order?

★ **Decisions! Decisions!**

- Which departments might receive a copy of an invoice and why?
  Yes, that's right:
- the accounts department for recording accounts and checking payments
- if goods were sold, the stores section or warehouse would need to record stock
- if goods were to be delivered the despatch department would need a copy

CHECKING AN INVOICE

When a customer receives an invoice, there are several points to be checked before it is passed for payment, viz:

1 Check goods have been received according to the order and note any discrepancy.
2 When invoices are received for services check that the service has been carried out.
3 Check all prices, ie price of goods, discounts and VAT.
4 Check calculations, for each item as well as the total.

E & O E

This means 'Errors and Omissions Excepted' and is printed on the invoice. This means that as far as the supplier is aware the invoice is correct except for errors and omissions. It

INVOICE						No 589

INVOICE

No 589

From: Bradford Superstores
Kings Road
BRADFORD
BD9 8PL

Tel: BRAD 234567

Telex: 55261 BRADSTORES

VAT Registration No 123 45678

Date: 26/2/8–

To:

> P Uttley Ltd
> Rawdon Road
> RAWDON
> RA5 3KM

Terms:

Completion of Order No A723 dated

Quantity	Description	Ref/ Cat No	Price each £	Cost £	VAT rate %	VAT amount £
2 week	Hire of stand 3' x 12' at the side of the north entrance to Bradford store	10-24 Feb	200 per week	400		
	Plus VAT			60	15	60.00
				460		
	E & O E					

Delivered on:
by:

Fig 57

gives the supplier the right to make an extra charge if he has made a mistake, eg an undercharge or has made an error in the addition.

★ **Decisions! Decisions!**

● **Why is it necessary to check an invoice before passing it on for payment?**

Trainee task 63 (a)

You have been passed these two invoices for checking. You are required to check these thoroughly noting any discrepancies.

The Sales Department has ordered various materials for a sales promotion drive, and has received this invoice. You are required to check the invoice to see if it is correct. The goods have been received.

INVOICE

No 789

From: Jarvis Stationers Ltd
         Daltrey Avenue
         BRADFORD
         BD10 41CJ
Tel: BRAD 9247   Telex: 55261 BRADSTORES

VAT Registration No 123 45678   Date: 25 February 19—

To: | BRADFORD SUPERSTORES
      | Kings Road
      | BRADFORD
      | BD9 8PL

Terms:

Completion of Order No 47392   dated   20/2/—

Quantity	Description	Cat No	Price each £	Cost £	VAT rate %	VAT amount £
2	Notice Boards 36" x 24"		22.50	50.00		
1	Notice Board 48" x 36"		31.50	31.50		
2 cartons	Storage Mailing Tubes		25.50	50.00		
				131.50		
	Less discount 10%			13.00		
	TOTAL			118.50		

E & O E

Delivered on: 23/2/—
by: Van

The invoice below is for shelves and drawers
in the sales office. The work has been carried
out.

INVOICE

No 91

From: Jenson Joinery Ltd
24 Kingswear Road
BRADFORD
BD17 4TR

Tel: BRAD 9462   Telex:

VAT Registration No 55261 BRADSTORES   Date: 25 February 19--

To:
Bradford Superstores
Kings Road
BRADFORD
BD9 8PL

Terms:

Completion of Order No 47399   dated 20/2/8-

Quantity	Description	Cat No	Price each £	Cost £	VAT rate %	VAT amount £
20 hrs	For fitting new shelving and drawers in Sales Office at above address					
	Labour @ £9 per hr		9	190.00		
	Plus VAT			30.00	15%	30.00
				220.00		
	E & O E					

Delivered on:
by:

As a special sales promotion drive Bradford Superstores have bought from France a new range of food mixers and blenders. The prices quoted are exclusive of VAT.

Product	Price exc VAT
Parisien A644 - Mini-chef hand held	£9.00
Parisien A645	£14.00
Parisien A646 – Mixer with liquidiser	£20.00
Parisien A647 Chef	£50.00
Coty top mix – hand held	£8.00
Midi C115 – hand held mixer	£9.00
Midi C155 – liquidiser + 2 bowls	£27.00
Thiers – Multi-chef	£25.00
Angex – Robot processor	£60.00
Angex – Master chef	£40.00

Trainee task 64 (a)

Using the VAT table, you are required to calculate the correct price for the goods listed above by adding 15% VAT to the prices given.

Gross		VAT	
£	p	£	p
1	00		15
2	00		30
3	00		45
4	00		60
5	00		75
6	00		90
7	00	1	05
8	00	1	20
9	00	1	35
10	00	1	50
20	00	3	00
30	00	4	50
40	00	6	00
50	00	7	50

SALES PROMOTIONS

Wide publicity is needed to maintain sales or to introduce new products so that customers are aware of the range of goods you sell. A product will rarely sell itself!

A good sales campaign depends upon five factors:

1 A good product at a competitive price.
2 Good market research to establish demand.
3 Good extensive advertising
4 Good salespeople to go out and sell the product.
5 Good and prompt delivery.

★ **Decisions! Decisions!**

● **How many ways can you think of advertising a product?
Yes, that's right.**

daily newspapers	radio
magazines	buses
trade papers	underground subways
posters	trade fairs
cinema	exhibitions
television	logos

PRESS RELEASE

In order to introduce a new product or a service, a **press release** is often sent out to newspapers or journals. (See Fig 58.)

Points to check when preparing a press release

● A heading or title is needed
● Important facts should appear at the beginning
● It should be written in the third person
● The name, address and telephone number should be stated of someone the Press can contact for further information
● The date should be specified when the article is to be published

Trainee task 65 (a)

You are required as part of your training to help draft a Press release for the opening of

---

ITALIAN WINE WEEK

Bradford Superstores are presenting an Italian Wine Week from Monday 4 March to Saturday 9 March at all their stores in the region.

Any customer buying pasta or Italian tomatoes will be invited to try a glass of the exceptional wines of Italy:

FRASCATI — a delicately fresh white wine from Rome
CHIANTI–CLASSICO — a full bodied red from the heart of Tuscany

In addition, the classic wines of Italy — BAROLO, BARBARESCO, SOAVE, ORVIETO, will be offered at special discount prices during the week.

———————

DO NOT release until 1 March
For further details, please contact Publicity Officer at Bradford Superstores

Fig 58

---

the new store in Headingley, Leeds. The person to contact for further information is Jane Cashmore, Publicity Officer, Sales Department, Bradford Superstores, etc. The information to be included is as follows:

'A new store is to be opened in Headingley, Leeds on Friday 1 March. This is a two-storey hypermarket designed in the same style as the continental hypermarkets. The store will be open six days a week. There will be two late night openings until 9 o'clock.

The Garden Centre will be open on Sunday, but will close on Monday.

A crèche is to be provided where children can be left while their parents shop. Car parking will be provided for up to 1,000 cars. There will be a self-service cafeteria and a restaurant. A special free bus service will be provided from the Central Bus station to the new store and back to town.

The opening ceremony will be performed by Mr Jack Shepherd the Managing Director at 9.30 am on 1 March

There will be special offers and discounts throughout the store in the opening week.'

★ **Memory jogger**

What are the points to check when drafting a Press release?

SALES FIGURES

Sales figures are collected from the stores at regular intervals and these figures are collated on one sheet at the end of the year so that the value of the total sales can be seen and comparisons made.

Listed in Fig 59 overleaf is an extract from the sales figures for 1984.

As part of your training you are required to be able to read and interpret figures. Consult the figures given and answer the following tasks.

Trainee task 66 (a)

a State which store had the highest sales.
b Which store had the lowest sales?
c Which store does not sell any wine?
d Which store does not have a kiosk?
e Which store sold the highest percentage of groceries?

Sales figures – January to December 1984					
Stores	1983–84 Actual sales	Departmental performance			
		Groceries	Non-food	Kiosk	Wines & Spirits
	£	%	%	%	%
Harrogate	2 500 000	66	9	15	10
Bradford	2 900 000	70	20	5	5
Peterborough	1 000 000	55	30	–	15
Grantham	1 400 000	62	24	10	4
Ipswich	1 750 000	68	18	7	7
Warwick	1 800 000	72	18	10	–
Staines	2 800 000	69	20	2	9
Skegness	1 400 000	55	25	15	5
Newbury	1 050 000	49	24	14	13
Blackpool	2 200 000	59	12	10	19
Scarborough	1 800 000	62	21	5	12
Stockton	3 900 000	71	19	5	5

Fig 59

f Which store sold the highest percentage of non-food goods?

g Which store sold the highest percentage of wine?

h What is the total amount of sales for the year 1984 for the branches shown?

SALES FORECASTING

From the annual sales figures, forecasts are made for the following year and stores are given a sales target to reach. This is the total amount of sales each store must try to achieve. It is estimated that sales will increase by 10% for the next year.

Trainee task 67 (a)

You are required to calculate the target sales figures for the stores listed in Fig 59.

★ **Memory joggers**

1 **Why are sales figures collated at regular intervals?**

2 **What is the sales target figure?**

PRESENTATION OF STATISTICS

Sales figures are often presented in a tabular statement as in Fig 59. However, there are other methods which may be used effectively.

Pie charts

A pie chart is a circle (in the shape of a round pie) divided into segments to illustrate proportions. A pie chart has greater visual impact. For example a pie chart could be used to illustrate the departmental performance of a store (Fig 60).

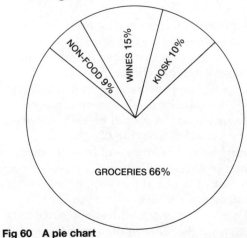

Fig 60   A pie chart

★ **Decisions! Decisions!**

● **What are the advantages of using a pie chart?**
● **What are the disadvantages?**
  Yes, that's right, it can only illustrate an approximate indication. It would be difficult to produce a pie chart if there were more than, say, eight segments.

Trainee task 68 (a)

Prepare two pie charts to illustrate the departmental performances for Peterborough and Bradford stores as shown in Fig 59.

Bar charts

An alternative method would be to use a bar chart. This is where figures or statistics are presented in a vertical or horizontal bar. They are similar to a pie chart in that they can illustrate an approximate indication. However, they do focus attention and present visual impact.

A bar chart might be used to compare figures. (See Fig 61.)

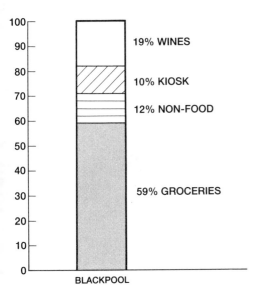

Fig 61   A bar chart

If more than one comparison is to be shown this is known as a **compound bar chart**.

★ **Memory joggers**

1 What is a pie chart?
2 What is a bar chart?
3 When might a bar chart be used?
4 What is a compound bar chart?

Trainee task 69 (a)

Prepare a bar chart to compare the departmental performance of Grantham and Skegness stores.

HOW COMPUTERS MIGHT BE USED IN THE SALES DEPARTMENT

A word processor might be used to prepare Press releases. The Press release could be drafted and any alterations could be quickly carried out without retyping.

A word processor could also be used for preparation and updating of sales literature and price lists.

Invoices can be prepared on the computer. Prices and details of goods may be stored in the memory on a database. The operator would key in the code or catalogue number and the quantity. The computer will calculate the costs per item.

The computer will also calculate the total cost. The computer may be programmed to calculate any discounts and VAT. It may also calculate the total sales for the day.

In addition the computer can be programmed to up-date stock.

Many computers now offer a graphics facility whereby charts and graphs can be produced visually on a VDU and a hard copy may be taken.

Many computers have a calendar function whereby all appointments are keyed in and can be seen instantly on the VDU. This would be very useful for sales representatives and could be used instead of the traditional diary.

CHECK YOUR PROGRESS

1 What is an invoice and what information does it contain?

2 Which departments might receive a copy of the invoice and why?
3 State five items to be checked before an invoice is passed for payment.
4 Explain what is meant by E & O E.
5 State five factors to be considered when planning a sales campaign.
6 List the various media which might be used to advertise a product.
7 List five points to check when preparing a Press release.
8 Explain what is meant by sales forecasting and sales targets.
9 Describe three methods of presenting statistical information.
10 List the duties of a trainee in the sales department.

Copy out and *tick* if you are able to:

- Check an invoice
- Prepare an invoice
- Calculate VAT
- Draft a Press release
- Interpret sales figures
- Calculate sales figures
- Present statistical data

10 OFFICE MACHINERY

As part of your training you are required to have practical experience and to use as much equipment as possible. Listed below are some of the equipment and machines you might find in any office:

- typewriters
- word processors
- computers
- calculators
- duplicators
- audio/dictating machines

TYPEWRITERS

Bradford Superstores has a range of typewriters:

- manual
- electric
- electronic

Manual typewriters

Is it only in the last few years that the sale of electric typewriters has been greater than those of manual typewriters. There are two sizes of machine:

1 A portable typewriter which can be carried quite easily.
2 A standard typewriter which is the most common model for general office work.

However, various sizes of carriages are available. Long carriages would be used for typing certain legal documents and for certain accountancy documents.

★ **Memory joggers**

1 **What are the three main types of typewriters?**

2 **What other equipment might be found in an office?**

Electric typewriters

Electric typewriters, both standard and portable, are now being used more frequently than manual machines. Many electric typewriters have extra facilities not found on manual typewriters, eg repeat keys, half-line spacing for corrections.

There are certain advantages in using an electric typewriter. These are:

1 It is less tiring for the operator to type. Therefore the typist can type at maximum speed for a longer time.
2 The electrically operated keys produce a light and even touch.
3 By adjusting the pressure control more carbon copies can be produced.
4 Electric typewriters are ideal for cutting stencils due to the sharp impression of the keys.

★ **Decisions! Decisions!**

- **Will the use of an electric typewriter result in an increased typing speed?**

Electronic typewriters

An electronic typewriter (Fig 62) has a conventional keyboard, plus special operational keys and a special memory unit. These typewriters can store characters in the memory as the operator types.

The basic electronic typewriter has a limited memory capacity of 15 characters.

Most basic electronic typewriters offer a 'line-by-line' facility whereby the material which the typist keys in is displayed in a small window and not on the paper. The typist may then correct the work on the screen which holds up to one typing line in length. When the operator is satisfied that the line is correct, this may then be printed out on the paper.

On most electronic machines it is possible to switch from elite to pica pitch at the touch of a key.

More sophisticated electronic typewriters have extensive memories – up to 60 000 characters can be stored. The memory can be used to store margin settings, standard phrases, standard paragraphs and standard letters. These machines have automatic facilities like centring, justification and automatic printing.

★ Decisions! Decisions!

- **What advantages are there in using electronic typewriters?**

Fig 62

WORD PROCESSING

This is an office automation facility which uses a computer processor to prepare, edit, store, retrieve and print written text. It comprises three parts:

1 A keyboard and a video terminal for inputting data.
2 A computer storage facility for storing data.
3 A printing device for printing data – this is the output.

(See Fig 63.)

Keyboard and VDU

The keyboard is similar to an electronic keyboard to which special operational keys have been fitted. Data is keyed in via the keyboard and the characters appear on the screen (this is called a VDU – visual display unit). The text can be checked and corrections made if necessary. The data is then stored on the computer.

Computer storage

Data may be stored on a 'floppy disk', a hard disk or a magnetic tape. Floppy disks can hold between 80 and 130 pages of A4 text. Hard disks can hold as much information as 100 or more floppy disks.

Printers

Text is keyed in via the keyboard, stored on the computer, checked and edited on the screen and it is only printed when the operator instructs the printer to do so. There are several printers on the market using different print units, eg golf-ball heads, daisy wheels, dot matrix. More expensive are ink jet printers and laser printers. The more expensive printers are faster and present a higher quality of print. (See Fig 64.)

★ Memory joggers

1 What are the three main components of a word processing system?
2 What is used to store data on a word processing system?
3 What advantages do ink jet and laser printers offer?
4 How much data can be stored on a floppy disk?
5 How much data can be stored on a hard disk?

Word processing may be organised in three ways

1 Stand alone system

This is the basic system of a keyboard, VDU, microprocessor and printer. This is known as a work station. The printer is separate. It is

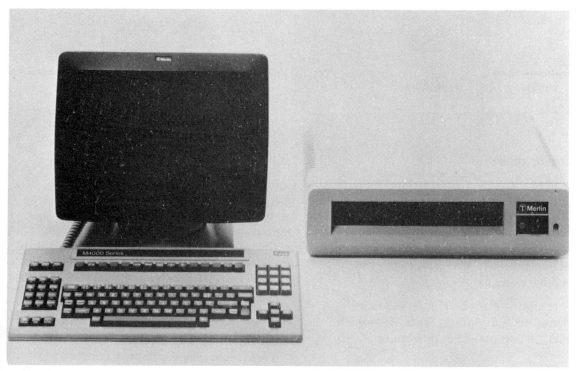

Fig 63

Fig 64

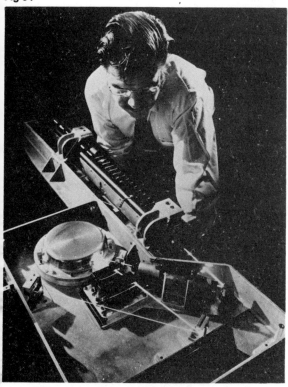

possible for two or more operators to share a printer, but each work station would have its own microprocessor to store data.

2 Shared logic system

Using a shared logic system a number of work stations share a central processor and a printer. Material is usually stored on hard disks and all operators have access to it. More than one printer may be used.

3 Word processing linked to data processing – network systems

Word processors are connected to central computers so that material can be used from database computer files as well as from the word processor. Terminals may be linked to the computer by cable or by means of communications through the telephone. It is thus possible to link one terminal to another several miles away.

★ **Memory joggers**

1 What is a stand alone system?
2 What is a shared logic system?

MICRO	TELEPHONE	MODEM	TELEPHONE	MICRO
1	2·	3	4	5

Fig 65

Electronic mail

Instead of using the traditional mail service of sending letters through the post many firms are now sending their mail through a system of communicating computers. Fig 65 illustrates how it works.

Each micro must be connected to the telephone network (1 ⟷ 2, 4 ⟷ 5).

The telephone must be connected to a **modem**. This is a computer machine which converts typed messages into sound.

Data is keyed into the terminal and can be sent via the telephone network and modem to terminal 5.

Uses of word processing

Word processors are useful for:

text editing
standard letters
standard paragraphs
updating text

★   Decisions! Decisions!

• **Can you suggest which departments in Bradford Superstores might use word processors and for what purpose.**

COMPUTERS

Computer systems can range from simple micros to highly sophisticated systems linking large main-frame computers and terminals, perhaps to other parts of the world.

However there are certain common features in all computer systems. (See diagram below.)

Uses of computers

Computers may be used for the following applications:

1   Files, records and data may be stored.
2   Orders and invoices may be calculated and printed.
3   Payroll can be calculated, stored and printed.
4   Stock can be controlled and up-dated.

★   Memory joggers

1   **What are the common features in all computer systems?**
2   **What is the CPU and what is its function?**
3   **How might data be input into the CPU?**

★   Decisions! Decisions!

• **For what purposes might Bradford Superstores use computers?**

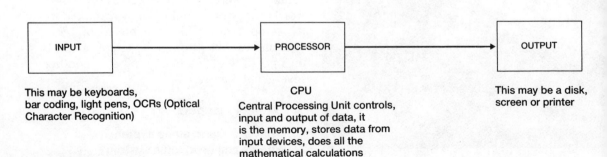

INPUT	PROCESSOR	OUTPUT
This may be keyboards, bar coding, light pens, OCRs (Optical Character Recognition)	CPU Central Processing Unit controls, input and output of data, it is the memory, stores data from input devices, does all the mathematical calculations	This may be a disk, screen or printer

REPROGRAPHY

Duplicating is the process whereby a master is prepared from which a number of other copies can be obtained.

Photocopying is a method of copying direct from the original. No master sheet needs to be prepared.

There are three methods of duplicating:

1 Spirit duplicating.
2 Stencil duplicating.
3 Offset-litho duplicating.

Spirit duplicating

This is mainly used in schools and colleges. It is not often used in businesses nowadays. The master is a piece of art paper, glossy on one side. A special hectagraphic carbon is placed to the glossy side and an impression is made by writing or typing on the master.

Three hundred copies can be obtained, but the image gets weaker. The quality of print is not very good. However, it is useful for producing small batches of internal communications and particularly useful when colours are used – one merely changes the carbon.

Stencil duplicating

The master is a special wax coated sheet. An impression is cut on the typewriter or by a special stylus pen. The stencil is then placed on to an ink cylinder on the duplicator and the ink is forced through the cuts.

Stencils can be pre-cut by manufacturers to any design the customer wishes. In addition an electronic scanner (see Fig 66) may be used which electronically cuts a stencil (including photographs and diagrams) by means of a photo-electric cell and a cutting stylus. The documents can then be reproduced on an ordinary stencil duplicator.

Stencil duplicating is suitable for producing price lists, circular letters, sales literature, minutes of meetings, reports, etc. Up to 7000 copies can be obtained from one stencil. Stencil duplicating does not require good

Fig 66

quality bond paper, instead cheaper absorbent copy paper may be used.

★ Decisions! Decisions!

- **What are the advantages to using stencil duplicating?**
The main disadvantage to stencil duplicating is that it is difficult and time-consuming to use different colours. The ink cylinder has to be changed, as each cylinder stores its own coloured ink, and a separate stencil has to be used for each colour.

Offset-litho

The cost of this equipment (see Fig 67) has been reduced considerably in the past few years and many firms are using offset as it is cheaper than using specialised printing services.

The offset master is produced on a paper or metal plate. The masters are normally prepared on an electrostatic plate-maker. This is a quick and easy process. It is possible to type on a paper master if a special greasy offset ribbon is used. It is also possible to produce a master on certain photocopiers.

Whilst a junior or trainee could learn to operate a stencil duplicating and a scanner quickly, a trained operator is required for an offset litho machine.

Offset-litho produces a high quality of reproduction. It is capable of producing a large number of copies – 5000 from a paper plate and up to 100 000 from a metal plate. It is particularly useful for forms, letterheads, sales leaflets, catalogues with photographs.

Fig 67

★ **Memory joggers**

What are the advantages to using offset litho?
Any disadvantages?

★ **Decisions! Decisions!**

- **What factors need to be considered when choosing a duplicator?**
  Yes, that's right:

- **cost**
- **how often it will be used**

- **what it will be used for**
- **quality of reproduction**
- **whether colours or photographs required**
- **whether a trained operator is required**

Copiers

Most modern offices now use electrostatic copiers (Fig 68). The electrostatic system developed in America is a 'dry' process, producing excellent quality copies.

Electrostatic copiers are normally flat-bed type, ie copies can be made from bound books. Offset litho masters can be prepared on certain machines.

The main advantages to using copiers is that a facsimile or exact copy is obtainable. There is no need to check the copy. The machinery is simple to use and can be operated by a trainee or a junior.

Fig 68